Eva & Cindy,
Hope you Enjoy,
Karen Kerry

# PRISM

Seeing the World Through the Hearts
of People with Special Needs

# PRISM

Seeing the World Through the Hearts
of People with Special Needs

# KERRY BOUDREAUX

iUniverse LLC
Bloomington

PRISM,
SEEING THE WORLD THROUGH THE HEARTS
OF PEOPLE WITH SPECIAL NEEDS

iUniverse books may be ordered through booksellers or by contacting:

iUniverse LLC
1663 Liberty Drive
Bloomington, IN 47403
www.iuniverse.com
1-800-Authors (1-800-288-4677)

Because of the dynamic nature of the Internet, any web addresses or
links contained in this book may have changed since publication and
may no longer be valid. The views expressed in this work are solely those
of the author and do not necessarily reflect the views of the publisher,
and the publisher hereby disclaims any responsibility for them.

Any people depicted in stock imagery provided by Thinkstock are models,
and such images are being used for illustrative purposes only.
Certain stock imagery © Thinkstock.

ISBN: 978-1-4917-1813-1 (sc)
ISBN: 978-1-4917-1814-8 (hc)
ISBN: 978-1-4917-1815-5 (e)

Printed in the United States of America.

iUniverse rev. date: 02/15/2014

# TABLE OF CONTENTS

# DEDICATION

I dedicate this book to all the parents and guardians in the world who are caring for children and individuals with special needs. Your unwavering commitment to the growth of their mind, body and spirit is essential to their happiness and success.

In loving memory of Mrs. Kaye Haas
and Marie "ReRe" Roof.
Two of the best role models ever to grace our presence.

# ACKNOWLEDGMENTS

This book would not have been possible without the sacrifices and commitments of so many people.

I first want to thank my editor, Jamie Mercer, who has pushed me and challenged every thought and word with one goal in mind; to make this body of work the best it can be.

I want to thank my good friend and writing mentor, Dr. Harold Kleinert. You, the reader, will get to know Harold throughout the book. I think you will agree his life's work has made a profound impact on a lot of people in so many special ways. Harold, your life's work has touched every word and thought on these pages. Thanks for that chance meeting on the pool deck over 12 years ago. You have been a blessing to me and my family.

Thank you to our two oldest daughters, Kala and Kelsey. You have blazed your own trails. You have been tremendous role models for your kid sister. Our family would not be what it is today without your hearts and souls. You both have grown into outstanding young ladies and I am so very proud.

Thank you to my parents, who have challenged me my entire life to be more than mediocre. Perfection was my father's goal in all that he did. Striving to be your best was the minimum requirement for my mother.

Thank you to my in-laws, Barbara and the late Adrian Roof. You have been an inspiration to me for over 35 years. I would not be the person I am today nor have the family that I have today were it not for you. Thank you for being that constant beacon of hope and security as your daughter and I have traveled through life together.

I owe a tremendous amount of gratitude to all those who contributed to this work. Several of you answered my requests for a narrative and reflection. Many simply shared your story through simple conversation which, for some reason, resonated with me and caused me to ponder and write. Your willingness to allow me to share your stories with others enables these words to continue planting kindness and understanding throughout the world. Others took the time to read unedited versions and offered valuable feedback.

Thank you to Ciara Thomas, who answered my call to design the cover. I know that you, as a young aspiring graphics designer, were a bit fearful that you wouldn't meet my expectations, but I want you to know that you far exceeded them. I knew that your love and compassion for Kate, coupled with your God—given abilities, would produce some amazing work. I hope people judge this book by its cover.

Lastly, I want to thank my wife, Karen. I married my best friend and that's the way it should be. Measured by dollars, we're not millionaires, but if we're measured by the love and commitment we have for each other and our family, I'm sure we have surpassed millionaire status. Thank you for allowing me, over the past two years, to put pen to paper and record my thoughts and ideas so that they may be shared with the hope of enriching others with a small bit of hope, joy and encouragement. This book has been completed, and my hope and desire is that "our book" will continue to be written for many years.

# FOREWORD

This is a rare book, for it is written by a dad reflecting over the course of his youngest daughter's life and the meaning of that life for himself, for his family and for all who have been touched by his child's life. That his youngest daughter has Down syndrome is a part of his story—but it is only *one* part, and it is hardly the most important part.

Even if you are like me, and have worked with children and adults with disabilities all your life, this book will open your eyes to new perspectives, new, "prisms," in which the light collects to make striking images of the people we love and enables us to see the world in a way we have not seen.

On its surface, this is a small book of simple stories, of being a husband to a loving wife and a dad to three daughters, one of whom happens to have entered the world with Down syndrome. The whole point of this father's book is that he embarks on a journey not of his own choosing—and as he takes us through the journey, the unexpected occurs.

The extraordinary becomes very much a part of the ordinary, while the uncertainty of the future becomes a promise filled with joy. The most mundane of moments—coming home from work and bedtime prayers—become gifts of grace. The unfolding of his family's lives brings into focus the clear and constant presence of God. It is, as C.S. Lewis would so aptly put it, a case of being, "surprised by joy."

These are stories meant to be read and to be considered. The reader is invited to think about things they may never have considered. The visible power of signs in our lives, the fact that nothing happens by chance (at least, not the important stuff) becomes clear as this dad's story unfolds. The fact that God has a plan for each of us (sometimes a plan we approach with fear, sometimes a plan we come to embrace and sometimes a plan that becomes quite humorous at its edges—because God, after all, is the inventor of humor) is reinforced on every page of this book.

Faith is the key to finding meaning and purpose in our lives. Our children are so much a part of that purpose, and our faith in their future and what they, in turn, will give back to the world, is an essential part of parenthood. It may be the most important part.

This book is much more than the story of a family whose youngest child has Down syndrome. It is, in the end, a treatise on fatherhood and the delicate balance of unconditional acceptance of our children's identity, aligned with the most profound expectations of all that they can become.

It is the realization that fatherhood holds a much deeper purpose, a much more profound role, than our world believes today. It is the kind of fatherhood that wants much more than success or security or achievements for our children—it is the kind of fatherhood that realizes that nothing is more important than ensuring that each of our children becomes what they are called to be in God's plan. This is Kerry's dream for all of his daughters; it is his dream for his youngest daughter, Kate, and it should be our own dream for all of our children. It is the great lesson of this book.

Harold L. Kleinert, Ed.D
Executive Director
Human Development Institute—University Center
for Excellence in Developmental Disabilities
Professor, Dept. of Rehabilitation Sciences, College
of Health Sciences, University of Kentucky

May 2013

# PREFACE

Several years ago I was asked to collaborate with the University of Kentucky's Human Development Institute on a project called Brighter Tomorrows, www.brightertomorrows.org. The completed work is a valuable resource for families who are told that their child has a disability.

My role was to write a brief reflection, a, "Life Glimpse," as we called it, on my family, and particularly my experiences with our youngest daughter, Kate, who has Down syndrome. Spending time on this project was fulfilling for a number of reasons. Most importantly, I knew I was going to be helping others work through the challenges of receiving a diagnosis.

There were two major challenges to this project. First, there were numerous topics or, "glimpses," I wanted to include, but I was limited to just one.

Second, my narrative was limited to just 500 words. Needless to say, I quickly exceeded the 500-word limit. I was finally able to condense my work down to the specified guidelines, but this project caused me to continue to reflect and write on my own.

It's been about eight years since that project was completed and I've received many compliments on my efforts. If my short, written reflection in the Brighter Tomorrows project made a difference in someone's life, quite possibly I could touch others by sharing some of my additional, "glimpses."

I share these insights with the intention of helping others better understand the diverse opportunities when blessed with a child who has a disability. It is intended for families who are expecting a child or have just received a child who has a disability, and for those who simply enjoy a good read.

I want to give you a perspective from a father who was living a simple and ordinary life, which I thought was far from typical, when his youngest daughter was born with Down syndrome.

It is extremely difficult to understand the, "whys," when you receive this type of diagnosis. Everyone seems to react and/or feel differently. One of the biggest questions is, "Is there a correct way to react or feel?"

There is one common reaction that I've found among all people who have received a diagnosis, and that's fear. This is very natural. I certainly had it, my wife had it, my parents had it, my in-laws had it and our friends had it. Our fear was of the unknown.

The only people I've found who don't have it are those who have already have a child with a disability. Their reaction is, "Congratulations on your baby!," when they learn of your special child. This struck me as very interesting and heightened my curiosity as to why they had such a spirited and positive outlook. I made it a point to seek out this wisdom and to gain a better understanding of their perspective.

Now, after 12 years of raising a child with a disability, I understand why, and I want to share it with you.

I have several goals here. First, if you are reading with the eyes of a new parent who has just received the news that your child has been diagnosed with a disability such as Down syndrome, congratulations! If you're feeling a bit overwhelmed and a bit fearful, that's quite all right; like I said before, it's perfectly normal. I will try to alleviate at least some of this fear and anxiety.

It might help you to see a positive perspective from someone who has experienced what you are encountering. You see, fear can paralyze you emotionally, spiritually and physically. Fear can cause undue anxiety and can greatly affect your health and well-being. Fear can keep you from being the best that you can be to your spouse and your existing family.

Reducing or eliminating your fear will go far in caring for yourself and your precious new baby. Reducing or eliminating your fear will unleash so many opportunities and possibilities for you and your child to grow and develop, and to touch and influence so many people in a positive light. My hope is that you will quickly see that people with a disability such as Down syndrome are in many ways no different from typical kids. To the contrary, they are very much alike.

Second, if you are a friend of someone who has a family member with a disability or a friend of someone with a disability, or maybe you serve as a volunteer assisting people with special needs, you may want to have the chance to peer through a different set of eyes; their eyes. Often there are small curiosities that, if better understood, would strengthen all our relationships. Seeing the world through the hearts and eyes of others can give us new perspectives on life, ones that we may never have the opportunity to experience otherwise.

I personally experienced this fear and trepidation of learning that someone who had just received the news that their newborn child was diagnosed with a disability. It was shortly after I graduated college and I learned that a high school friend and his wife had just been given the news that their newborn son had Down syndrome. I remember the way the person delivered the news and I also remember the way I reacted to it. It was like a breaking news story of a catastrophic event.

"Did you hear about their son?"

"No, what about him?"

"He has Down syndrome!"

"Oh my goodness, what are they going to do!?"

I recently visited with a college student, Ciara, who told me about her experience with her soccer team and volunteering at a recent Buddy Walk event in Savannah, Georgia, a fundraiser for the local National Down syndrome Association Chapter. She had helped us several years ago with our Buddy Walk here in Lexington, Kentucky, and was familiar with families and people with Down syndrome. Her teammates, on the other hand, were not. When they agreed to their community service project, many of them were quite fearful and apprehensive. How do you to interact with the kids? What types of affection should you show?

These thoughts, questions and reactions are perfectly natural. Because of my personal experience with Kate, my thoughts, words and perceptions are totally different. If you were to ask Ciara's teammates if they enjoyed their day at the Buddy Walk and are their thoughts, feelings and emotions different because of it, I would venture to guess they would say yes. I'm confident they would, as Ciara said it was a life-changing experience for many of them. We all now see from a totally different view point. I see it as a parent of a child with a disability; Ciara and her teammates see it from the standpoint of being able to spend a day volunteering with people with Down syndrome.

My final goal is to provide those interested, with the opportunity to see the world through the heart of someone with special needs. Many people have met someone with Down syndrome, autism, etc., but they don't actually **know** them. My hope is this that this book gives them, though briefly, an intimate view into the lives of people with special needs so they can better understand themselves and their friends who may have a diagnosis.

Thank you for allowing me to share my experiences and take you on this short journey. I think you will find it enlightening, heart-warming and entertaining. I hope you enjoy reading the book as much as I enjoyed writing it.

# FIRST, LET'S GET TO KNOW EACH OTHER

We are a typical family. We're not perfect and we have the same challenges as most. I couldn't have said that several years ago. You see, that's one of my perceptions that has changed. Several years ago, I would have told you that we are a *very* different family, simply because we have a child with a disability. But that just isn't true.

We live and experience many of the same things as a typical family. We take family vacations, we have our four-bedroom home in the suburb, we go to church, we labor through the science projects, spend countless hours at the extracurricular activities, and on and on. We just aren't that different from a typical family. In fact, I would say we are a typical family!

My wife Karen and I met as we were beginning high school in 1979. Her father was in real estate and had developed a small subdivision. My parents purchased one of the lots there and built a house, which we called home from my early teenage years until I moved out of the nest. Being that Karen's father owned the subdivision, they opted to do the same. They built a home just a few doors down from us.

Living next door to each other (God said love thy neighbor as thy self, right?) and going to school together gave us a lot of time to become friends. Karen has two siblings, a brother and a sister, and a large extended family. As typical Southern families, there were plenty of family get-togethers, especially on Sundays. I was invited to attend with her family and her with mine. Many afternoon hours were spent eating home-cooked Southern country meals. Early evenings were passed with card games and pitching washers. We still look back on the days, some 30 years ago, with the fondest of memories.

Karen and I began dating a bit in high school, but it wasn't until our junior and senior years that we thought there may be something special about our relationship.

Our post high school educational years were spent apart. She was a year ahead of me in school and the first to go to college, attending Murray State University, which is about a 45-minute drive south from our hometown of Paducah, Kentucky. I went to Southern Illinois University, which is about a 90-minute drive in the opposite direction.

Back then there was no e-mail, social media, text messaging and the like. Today our kids are amazed at how we stayed in touch with "snail mail" letters and those once-a-week phone calls on Sunday evenings (when the rates were the lowest), and the occasional weekend visit.

During our four undergraduate years, we were able to stay very close and our relationship continued to grow. As we both neared completion of college, we sensed that we were, "Mr. and Mrs. Right," and the possibility of getting married was a bit more real. As I neared graduation, we announced our engagement and started planning our life together. We married in August of 1987, just two weeks after my graduation.

Now, Karen comes from a very successful athletic family. Her father, along with four of his brothers, played professional baseball. Karen was fortunate enough to adopt this great athletic ability, but her athletic days were cut short by a severe leg break when she was 16. I was a decent athlete as well, playing baseball and basketball in high school, and had the privilege of going to college on a baseball scholarship. I often joke that yes, I did marry for love, but the genetic pool was a close second. Everyone envisioned a group of boys, all following in their forefather's footsteps and becoming professional athletes.

God, however, had his own plans and blessed us with three daughters, none of whom was very interested in athletics!

We settled in Paducah, reconnecting with our roots after being away for four years of college. Our rich Southern tradition of Sunday family gatherings was restored. Evenings out with old and new friends in our small, western Kentucky river town were anticipated each and every week. Life was grand and couldn't be better.

But, as life goes, doors to new opportunities and growth open. In 1990, we received a great career opportunity which required a move to Memphis, Tn. It was one of the hardest decisions we have ever made, but we made it with the intention of one day returning to our beloved Paducah.

It didn't take us long to settle in to Memphis; it's a great town. It's a lot like Paducah; a river town boasting wonderful comfort cooking and food, and great Southern hospitality. The Southern charm was just like home. The river city blues music was vintage and made Memphis unique. And of course, there's Elvis; you can't live in Memphis without getting to know the King.

Karen and I found ourselves calling Memphis, "home." Both our careers were beginning to blossom and we were very involved in church. And it was there in Memphis, in 1991, that Karen gave birth to our first child, Kala.

Once again, as life goes, we were summoned down a new path. A great career opportunity to move into management came along but it required relocating to St. Louis, Missouri. The large, Midwestern town on the Mississippi River, mind you, was, and still is, one of our favorite cities, so we felt good about the move. With our love for sports, the city's strong faith community its wonderful people, we felt it was an ideal town for us to raise a family.

Soon after we moved our family grew once more with the birth of our second child, Kelsey, in 1993. We moved out of our small, two-bedroom apartment and bought our first house. As with most growing families, we had the tough decision of whether Karen would stay in the workforce or stay at home to raise the family. We opted for neither—she worked part-time. For us, we were living the American dream—a four-bedroom home in the suburbs, a two-car garage, a nice yard, a dog and two young toddler girls in tow. Just like Memphis, it didn't take us long to start calling St. Louis home. Once again, life was grand and couldn't be better. Games at the ole' ballpark, the incredible Italian food, family outings to the famous St. Louis Zoo, Grant's Farm and the Magic House, were all trappings for a great life.

As life goes though, we were faced with another great career opportunity with yet another promotion up the corporate food chain. But, like before, we were being asked to relocate, this time to Nashville, Tennessee.

Yes! Once again, we were back in the South. Just like Paducah and Memphis, we were greeted with Southern charm and hospitality. We grew fond of the great music that could be found on any street corner, pub or lunch time eatery.

"People-watching" was a hobby as you never knew who you were going to meet. Country music stars stay close to their roots and family, which means they shop and dine at the same places you and I frequent. It was fun to race back home and talk about who you saw at the grocery.

In 1999, four years after moving to Nashville, it seemed life turned a bit tipsy for us. We found out we were expecting our third child, which was fantastic news. Kala and Kelsey were eight and six, both in school and loving all that is life. I was working and traveling quite a bit and Karen was working part-time. Four months into her pregnancy Karen decided to quit her job to focus on her health and the family. Once again, life was grand and couldn't be better. Now for the tipsy part; just after we made the decision for Karen to quit work, I was notified that I was losing my job due to a major downsizing. So here we were, four months pregnant, a two-week severance package, Christmas just 45 days away, little savings and no income. What were we going to do?

## ... And Along Comes Kate

As the 21st century rolled in, so did many blessings. I landed a job and Karen's pregnancy was going well. What seemed like the longest four months ended with a tremendous blessing of a job and, in just another month, we would welcome another glorious blessing.

We enjoyed the usual pomp and circumstance with baby showers, fixing up the nursery and the like. Having two other daughters, was an especially fun and heartwarming experience for all of us. Kala and Kelsey were old enough to know and understand all that was going on. It was fun to watch them process all the excitement, to see them touch their mother's belly and feel their new baby sister move and wiggle inside. They still talk about it as if it were just yesterday.

As I said earlier, there was nothing unusual about our pregnancy. Checkups and doctor visits went as planned and without any concerns or issues. As with our previous kids, Karen didn't deliver on her due date and was admitted for induced labor. We spent the evening in the hospital with a slow induced labor, but still there was nothing out of the ordinary during the process. We had done this twice before and felt like old pros; all was calm. Frequent phone calls were made (text messaging and social media weren't the norm yet) to family members, giving them updates on the progress.

The only complication that came was near the end of labor. When Karen would have a contraction, Kate's heart rate would plummet. After 12 hours of induced labor, Kate was born on the morning of March 25, 2000. That's when normal left the building . . . with Elvis.

Immediately after Kate's birth, the doctor informed us there was a strong possibility that Kate had Down syndrome. She said they wanted to confirm it with a genetic test, but they were quite certain of their diagnosis. It was a bit of a shock, to say the least, but for some reason we were not overwhelmed by the revelation—and to this day, I'm not sure why.

I think one of the reasons is that both Karen and I had a good understanding of Down syndrome. I had childhood friend, Tommy (whom I will speak of later) who had Down syndrome, and a good friend and classmate of mine had a brother, Tim (I'll also speak of him later as well), with Down syndrome. Karen and I also volunteered at the annual Lion's Club Telethon, which helps provide the financial support for therapies and educational opportunities for people with different needs in Western Kentucky.

Karen has never wavered or questioned why Kate was born with Down syndrome. Oh, I think she questions why in a good and positive way, but not in the, "Why me, Lord, why have you given me this cross to bear?," kind of way. A few days after Kate's birth Karen shared an experience she'd had before Kate was born. Now, neither one of us are so-called conventional readers of the Bible. Many times we will simply pick up the Bible, randomly open it and read the passage, and then apply it to our day or to a particular situation.

Well, a week before Kate was born Karen couldn't sleep and woke up at 4 a.m. It was one of those Bible-opening moments, so she quietly reached for her Book and randomly opened it as she had done so many times before. As the pages parted, her fingers fell upon Mark 9:37 which reads, "Whoever receives a child such as this in My name, receives Me, and whoever receives Me receives not only Me but the One who sent Me." We've never forgotten that moment and we use it as a foundation for our love and acceptance of not only Kate, but all children.

Shortly after Kate's birth, we moved to Lexington. We settled into the community, getting involved in church, neighborhood and extracurricular activities, and school. There was a small Down syndrome organization, which we embraced as our new support group and extended family. Our new nest quickly took shape, making for a great home to raise our kids.

# MY WIFE, THE MOTHER
# OF OUR CHILDREN

As I've mentioned, Karen and I were high school sweethearts, but more importantly, we were also best friends. Our dating relationship was casual as our educational endeavors took us in separate directions; she to Murray State University and I to Southern Illinois University.

It has been close to 30 years of combined courtship and marriage. Yes, she was and still is very beautiful and attractive, but there's something more. That, 'something more,' is what I would describe as selflessness.

Karen has always been the one to always think of the other person first. Whether it is her family, friends or neighbors, they can rest assured that she is either working for them, thinking about them or praying for them. Karen seems to always have others' best interest at hand. Countless times over the years Karen has sacrificed her time and given of herself to others.

This selflessness has been and is the one trait that is most needed when raising a family of any kind, but it is most critical when you have a child with a disability. Selflessness sometimes means you have to make sacrifices, but most often it simply means that you have to redirect your goals, ambitions, actions and thoughts to other areas and facets of life that you had not planned to pursue. Is it hard and challenging? Yes, absolutely. Is it impossible to accomplish? Absolutely not.

Karen's selflessness has enabled her to impact our family and community in countless ways. Our family has benefitted as she has chosen to stay home and raise our daughters. We've been blessed that she wanted to do this as I think our family is much healthier because of her efforts.

Having a child with a disability requires much more attention and care from the mother. If you don't have the adequate family support it can negatively impact your well-being.

As with most new mothers, Karen was fully committed to providing Kate with all the necessary love and attention. Not once has she flinched at the thought of raising a child with a disability. Every ounce of her heart and soul is poured not only into Kate, but her entire family. Not once has she shied away from the diagnosis. Maybe she's never had anything to shy away from because she's never seen Kate and our family as the diagnosis.

Karen has been a guiding light for anyone who comes into her sphere. She has worked too many volunteer jobs and hours to mention them all here. She has mentored and guided students and young professionals in their educational journeys and careers. She has assisted countless new moms and families who have just received a diagnosis that their child has Down syndrome. She has counseled families in rural and depressed areas in terms of child and healthcare needs, and she has counseled families who have lost a loved one with Down syndrome.

Karen has always had a unique perspective on Kate and raising a child with a disability. Some of it may be learned, but I firmly believe it's her innate nurturing coupled with a mother's natural love for her child.

Karen recently shared with me the following reflection and agreed to allow me to share it with you.

*As I sit here reflecting on our lives over the years, I realize how blessed I am in so many ways. It becomes apparent I was being prepared by all my experiences and people in my life along the way. From birth, my family gave me the faith in God, taught me the importance of being true to oneself and taught me the priorities in life—God, family, work and service. By following the example of my parents, Adrian and Barbara Roof, and extended family, it has helped me to stay grounded in my faith and understanding of God's hands in our lives.*

*Growing up in a small faith community of St John in Paducah, Kentucky, you feel the roots of love and faith with all those you meet. It was during my childhood there that I learned about loving unconditionally and accepting everyone as perfect, the way God made them. The culture of our community was to embrace children with Down syndrome or other disabilities as they did everyone else, because of our faith in God's plan and it's what our families did.*

*Little did I know I would be leaning on those experiences 30 years later. Since we didn't know prenatally Kate had Down syndrome, the first moment I saw her precious little face, I got cold chills from head to toe. I felt the same spirit of love and joy as I reflected on the wonderful families and friends from my childhood past. None of the families would have been the same without their child or sibling with Down syndrome. God had put them in our lives for a reason; to show us how to love unconditionally!*

*Kerry and I hold these values with our family. We have been blessed with three incredible daughters, all gifted and talented, to love and nurture. Kala and Kelsey have done a fabulous job as big sisters by loving, teaching and being terrific role models for Kate. They have taught her how to crawl, walk, speak, swim and dance. They teach her to be genuinely nice to others. They model this as they encourage, cheer and believe in her abilities.*

*Now, she introduces herself to others with a firm hand shake and always has a compliment for them. Whenever someone has a good performance, Kate is there with a high five. It's as if she has appointed herself as everyone's official cheerleader.*

*As I observe her in school, dance class, swim practice, cheerleading, soccer, piano or guitar class, I see a young adolescent girl with the same hopes and dreams as her sisters and other peers. She has the same look in her eyes as she works hard and accomplishes her goals. There is always time for "happy" dance when something great is accomplished! I can honestly say she is a focused young girl, and knows what she does and doesn't want. She has been involved in church, school and the community and now expects the same from everyone else.*

*As we appreciate the present moment we are in, I wish I could freeze time in some ways because I absolutely love where we are right now. However, I look forward to living our lives and experiencing the joys and triumphs for all of us in the days and years to come. The lessons we have learned from the past have taught us to see the goodness in everyone, and the spirit of who they are and the role they have in our lives. If we only see people through "man's eyes" then it would appear that some don't measure up. However, if we choose to see people and situations through "God's eyes", you see a different reflection. You see the happiness in their smile, eyes, embrace, steps and attitude. Keep the spirit ALIVE, see God's REFLECTION, and REFLECT it to those around you!!*

# WHAT IS DOWN SYNDOME?

So what is Down syndrome? I think this can be answered from two perspectives. First, medically, it's pretty easy to answer and is fairly straightforward. There are numerous articles and books written on this subject which you can reference at your leisure, but I will attempt to give you a brief explanation here. The second perspective is from a parent and also from someone who has Down syndrome, and is not quite as straightforward.

Medically speaking, Down syndrome is a genetic condition which is determined at the point of conception. Each person has 23 sets of chromosomes, which determine our physical traits. Someone with Down syndrome has an extra copy of the $21^{st}$ chromosome. Approximately one in 1000 people is born with it. It doesn't discriminate between nationalities, races or gender; all human beings have an equal chance of contracting this condition. There is no cure as it's not a disease nor is it contagious.

Down syndrome does bring certain physical characteristics. Someone with Down syndrome has beautiful, round, almond-shaped eyes. They're typically shorter in stature and tend to have a bit less muscle tone, which allows them to be extremely flexible, which makes them great gymnasts. Kate has the unique ability of being able to clasp her hands behind her back, then raise her arms up and over her head without unclasping her hands. It's a cool trick very few other people can pull off.

People with Down syndrome tend to have a slightly smaller mouth. Many people think that their tongues are larger, which is an understandable myth as their smaller mouths gives the appearance of a larger tongue. This particular trait presents some challenges with their speech; however, with proper speech therapy, someone with Down syndrome can develop excellent speaking and communication skills.

There are some intellectual differences as well. Many years ago, it was thought that people with Down syndrome simply could not learn due to the lack of the necessary memorization skills and abilities. What we have found through research and working with those with Down syndrome is that their brains simply process information differently. Reading, writing and arithmetic can be mastered. Oh, it takes a bit more practice and repetition, and different methods of teaching, but it can be done.

Can it be mastered at the highest level? Who knows? What we have learned is that each individual has his/her own unique ability, determination and attitude, and like all other people, these factors determine how much they can accomplish and how far they can travel. Today, we feel we have only seen the tip of the iceberg in terms of what people with Down syndrome can accomplish.

People with Down syndrome sometimes have additional medical issues. Some have gastrointestinal concerns which require a slightly altered diet. Some may have a heart murmur which may require surgery. Some may require hearing assistance or eyeglasses at an early age.

As for Kate, she has experienced most of the above issues and concerns. School is a challenge, but not impossible, as we have found some wonderful instructors, teachers and tutors who have introduced some very unique and 'Kate-specific' teaching aids and methods.

She had a slight heart murmur but no surgery was required. She requires glasses, which she enjoys wearing. She recently got braces and loves to change their colors at each checkup. All in all, she living a simply, ordinary life much like her peers are doing.

Now, on to the second perspective . . .

# MY FIRST FRIEND WITH DOWN SYNDROME

Around 1979-80, Karen's uncle, Phil Roof, started raising veal cattle on his farm in Western Kentucky. His in-laws, Mr. and Mrs. Klemenz, and their son Tommy, lived and worked on the farm. Tommy had Down syndrome and was 15 or 16 years old at the time.

I was just finishing up middle school and went to work doing odd jobs for Phil as a young, wirier farm hand. It was while I was working on the farm that I first met Tommy and his parents. This was my first relationship with someone with Down syndrome.

Tommy and I got to know each other quite well over the years; some would say we were best friends. Tommy was boisterous and had a deep laugh. He stood about five feet tall and weighed in at about 145 lbs. He loved to sing, but like me, couldn't carry a tune in a bucket.

Like most close friends our friendship grew through working beside one another and just spending lazy country afternoons together. Our days started out at 4:30a.m. with the first feeding of the cattle. Tommy and I worked the feeding buckets while Phil distributed the feed and managed the 'boys.'

We would finish up by 10 a.m., leaving a couple of hours to take care of the other chores around the farm before our noon meal and some down time. I call it a meal and not a lunch for a reason. Aunt Marie and Mrs. Klemenz cooked a full meal for us each day; pot roast, green beans, carrots and potatoes with brown gravy and homemade biscuits were the norm. It was not lunch, it was a meal.

Afternoons were meant for a little rest and relaxation, country style. Tommy and his parents raised a few chickens, so I would help tend to them. We had a couple of old horses that provided some fun for us, especially when we tried to ride them bareback. A small, stocked pond offered some nice afternoon fishing as well as an occasional splash ourselves. A wild blackberry patch on the back of the farm was always worth the trip as a big harvest meant fresh blackberry cobbler. These were, as they say, the good ole days.

Tommy was hard working and was a stickler for detail and proper procedure. He had a particular feeding process and if I tried to circumvent it, he would let me know about it. It was a kind first reminder but the second wasn't as nice. I admit that on occasion I intentionally broke procedure just to get a rise out of him. We had a lot of fun together.

I remember being fearful at first as to how to treat and communicate with Tommy. My fear was soon dispelled as I saw how his family treated him. Their expectations for him were no different than they were for anyone else. He was expected to do the best to his ability—nothing less, nothing more. He was also expected to honor God and treat people with respect.

Tommy's parents shared with me a story that I will never forget. When Tommy was born, the doctors encouraged them to turn Tommy over to the state as they felt someone else could better care for him. Now at the time, this was pretty enticing. It was the 1960's, and medical knowledge regarding Down syndrome was not very advanced. There was no research on therapy intervention and there was no home healthcare.

The medical community was of the belief that people with Down syndrome could not retain knowledge and had a very limited learning capacity; hence, they would simply not be productive to society. It was assumed that it was a futile effort to teach them anything as they could not retain the knowledge.

15

Well, Mr. and Mrs. Klemenz and their doctor however, were way ahead of their times on this issue. Owning a small farm in central Kentucky, there wasn't much money to go around, but one thing they did have was love for their children, no matter what the condition. They told me all Tommy needed was unconditional love and there was no way they were going to give him up for someone else to rear. With the encouragement and advice of their physician, the help and graces of their family and community, Tommy was loved and his needs were cared for by his own family.

Even with Tommy's disability, I quickly found that he was much like a typical person. He had emotions, he loved it when he played games, got excited when his favorite teams won and get mad when they lost.

Tommy and I were close. Little did I know that God put Tommy in my life for more than just having another friend. He put Tommy in my life at an early age to prepare me and to give me a better understanding of what I was going to experience 25 years later. He knew I was going to need the special wisdom that Tommy was giving me.

Tommy recently died with his family at his side. I miss Tommy. I'll never forget the great times we had and the close bond that we created. He was special; not only to me but to everyone. I keep his obituary close at hand to help me remember what he meant to us all. Below is a short excerpt which describes Tommy much better than I could ever attempt to.

*. . . Snowbound during one of the most severe winter storms of 1961, Magdelen delivered Tommy and Greg(Tommy had a twin brother) at the family's isolated dairy farm without the help of a doctor; only aided by her 19 year old daughter, Marie, a nursing student at the time. The twins' newsworthy birth made the headlines the very next day in the Louisville papers and from that day forward, Tommy, blessed with the gift of Down syndrome,*

*continued forward in his remarkable life, surprising friends and family and making all who got to know him smile.*

*Advised by their family doctor to love him and raise him like they did with their other children, the Klemenz' did just that and so Tommy, "the Doopster" as he was affectionately known by his dad, began his life of being loved and of giving love. He had loads of common sense, held his own with household chores, helped with the animals on his parents' dairy farm and was always up for a good joke,—'hypnotizing' people was his specialty.*

*When he was older, he attended schools in Louisville and participated wholeheartedly in the Special Olympics. After his studies were complete and his parents retired, the three of them moved to Paducah to live with his sister, Marie and her family on their farm. There he worked alongside his sister 'ReRe' and her husband, Phil, and their daughters. Always conscientious, Tommy was never late to help with the farm chores and feeding the animals.*

*Tommy was a member of the St. John Evangelist Catholic Church for over twenty years and it was there that he received his First Communion. Both he and his father participated in the Western Kentucky Right-to-Life movement, even winning an award one year for their involvement.*

*Tommy was a big sports fan who loved bingo, the Three Stooges, and UK basketball, and baseball. He was creatively masterful at charades, consistently brought down the house with his enthusiasm and dramatic rendition of 'The National anthem', and loved rooting for any winning team. Tommy often switched sides during the 4$^{th}$ quarter or in the bottom of the 9$^{th}$ to ensure his passionate cheerleading and allegiance stayed with the victors. No one ever minded the switch as he was as entertaining as the game itself. After the Final Four, he always bought a* *t-shirt of the winning team to proudly display that he too was a winner, and no one disputed it.*

*At Christmas no one opened presents better than Tom. Two-liter bottles of coke, definitely not Pepsi, were one of his favorite presents. He, being who he was, was a gift back to the giver, making them feel spectacular because of his surprise, thankfulness and childlike wonder.*

*After the death of both of his parents, Tommy, at the age of 26, officially moved in with his sister, 'ReRe', her husband Phil Roof, a professional baseball player, and their four daughters. For the next almost twenty years, Tommy lived out a sports fanatics dream traveling across the country in time for Spring Training, and following Phil's team to wherever it took them. Tommy was each team's unofficial mascot and biggest fan. No one rooted more boisterously and no one felt the losses harder than Tommy. In the locker room, he always lifted the spirits of the players encouraging them in his own way that 'we would get them tomorrow'. He never met a stranger as he called everyone his 'buddy'.*

I think and pray for his guidance often, asking him to give me wisdom and understanding with Kate. I know he's there, watching over me and helping me provide Kate with the love and patience needed to best nurture her talents and abilities. I know he's there, extending his loving hand to Kate as well, to guide and teach her how to care for others.

*Tommy and me at his first communion*

# GETTING INVOLVED
# AND ADVOCATING

While we were in Nashville, we utilized the Middle Tennessee Down Syndrome Association to gather information, resources and support. Kate was just a few months old when they held their annual conference, so the timing couldn't have been more perfect for us to get involved with them. We gained so much insight into therapy opportunities, teaching aids, play groups, counselors, estate planning specialists and more from not only this conference but from all the resources that the association provided.

As I mentioned earlier, Lexington had a small support group, The Down Syndrome Association of Central Kentucky (DSACK), but nothing formal had been established. Caroline, a high school classmate of mine, lived in Lexington, and I knew her oldest daughter had Down syndrome. We quickly connected with Caroline, and started our networking. In 2001, we attended some support group meetings and met some wonderful people, who are still our friends today.

Karen and I inquired about developing a more formal organization and asked if there would be enough support for it. Caroline and others agreed that a more formal group was needed, so we decided to pool our talents to make it happen. Karen has great leadership skills and this was all she needed. We were blessed to have her as a full-time Mom so the time and energy needed to start this project was not a major issue. Karen rallied those who were willing to help and the process of building a larger, more vibrant organization began.

The goal and mission of the organization was to provide resources regarding Down syndrome to expecting and new parents and their families. In addition, we wanted to provide another voice for not only those with Down syndrome, but people with special needs in general. We wanted to advocate on their behalf, but more importantly we wanted to assist them in being self-advocates; yes, the best advocate is a self-advocate. We wanted them to have a voice in their schools, churches and communities.

Advocacy can be quite a challenge, but ultimately, very rewarding. At its core, advocating requires a deep and strong passion for your mission and vocation. It often requires lots of both volunteering and commitment. Because you most likely are personally involved, advocating can and will become emotionally charged. I say this in a good light as you can't help but get emotional when you are working to improve the lives of those you love. Those emotions will run the entire gamut, from joy and happiness, and from anger and disappointment.

Before I go further, I want to discuss a point here—one that makes a huge difference in the success of one's advocating efforts on behalf of someone with special needs. Whether from the standpoint of a large organization, parent or self, this must be kept in mind at all times. ***You are advocating, not fighting.***

You are advocating or speaking on behalf of someone who needs an additional voice. You are not fighting, you are advocating—so don't call it a fight. This is not cancer or some other dreadful disease. This is not the latest "war" on something that has to be stopped, so don't fight.

So why do I feel this way? Why do I make such an implored plea? The moment you say you are fighting for their rights or fighting for their cause, whoever you are working with automatically goes into defense mode. Their shields go up and their weapons are drawn, figuratively speaking. Suddenly a mental barrier is erected that must be crossed.

The attitude of working together has been diminished, if not completely lost. It's easy to fall into this trap, especially if we feel the "war" was started by the other party, such as the school, government or employer.

From my experience, the true intent of everyone with whom we have worked has always been Kate's best interest. Have there been times when we've had disagreements and differences of opinion? Absolutely. What we have tried to do is work together to come up with an amicable solution that fits within everyone's framework.

Ok, so where was I? Oh yes, back to DSACK. The first order of business was to establish the organization's non-profit status, so money could be raised. The United Way graciously allowed us to "piggyback" on their organization, so Step One was quickly completed. The next order of business was to find some people that understood our needs and had a passion for our kids and families to help lead the new organization.

Being in Lexington, these people were not hard to find as Lexingtonians are well known for their commitment to others and their community. The people we found were first class and a perfect fit.

Our first advisory board consisted of a special education teacher, an attorney, a university professor, a pediatrician, a physical therapist and local business leaders. They were so instrumental in developing the vision and mission of the organization.

One individual was and still is a very special person, Dr. Harold Kleinert. Harold, as we call him, was put in our path by the graces of God. At the time, only a couple of people within the organization knew him and his department at the University of Kentucky. He was a quiet researcher (but quite the social chatter box when you get to know him) and director of the Human Development Institute (HDI) at UK. The Institute focuses on providing learning and advocating opportunities for people with disabilities.

Karen and Harold were volunteering one evening at our neighborhood swim meet when they met for the first time.

Harold has spent his life advocating and researching on behalf of people with both physical and intellectual disabilities. His absolute passion and love of people with special needs is displayed in his entire life's body of work. His leadership and dedication was exactly what we needed. Shortly after this initial meeting with Karen, Harold agreed to be on the board.

So, now what would we call our newfound organization. The group decided to keep the original name, then solicited a local marketing firm to help with a logo.

But in order for the organization to fulfill its mission, we needed some financial resources. We had already started that process by contacting the National Down Syndrome Association about possible fundraising opportunities. They recommended we hold a local Buddy Walk, where people gather for a morning or afternoon of games and activities. As with a typical charity walk, money is raised through a registration fee and sponsorships.

So, it was decided; we would host the first Lexington Buddy Walk as our first big fundraiser. Many people took charge of committees and volunteers stepped forward. It was absolutely incredible how the community stood behind us in support for our kids.

From the start, we wanted the Buddy Walk to be a day of celebration for the kids with Down syndrome and their families— this was at the heart and core of our foundation and thinking. We see these kids as people, not the diagnosis. We see them for their possibilities and not for their limitations, just the same as everyone else.

The first annual Buddy Walk was held in Lexington in September of 2002. Keeneland, the country's premier horse racing course, was chosen as the location.

I will never forget it. The walk was to start at 9 a.m. It rained all morning and we were trying to decide if we should cancel the event. The executive decision was made that the show must go on. At about 8:15 a.m. the weather dramatically changed as it went from a temperature of 50 degrees and raining to sunny skies and 60 degrees. It couldn't have been a more perfect day.

We had pony rides, face painting, arts and crafts, inflatable games, fire trucks, a helicopter landing and more. The first Buddy Walk raised close to $20,000. In 2012 we celebrated our 10th anniversary of the Buddy Walk, and we raised over $120,000 in one day.

After several years leading the group, Karen stepped aside to allow other talents and ideas to be part of the organization. Karen stayed on as an advisory board member, helping to guide the overall mission and direction.

DSACK has grown into more than we ever imagined. What started out as a support group with a small lending library, a summer picnic and a pot luck Christmas party has blossomed into so much more.

Today, DSACK funds monthly outings for the kids. There's an awareness campaign where parents share with community organizations and schools what Down syndrome is and how someone with it is affected. There's an annual one-day continuing education conference for parents, educators and professionals, attended by over 100 people. DSACK also works with the medical community with outreach programs for new and expecting parents.

DSACK could not be what it is today if not for the many people who started it, and also for the many people who have continued its work. It continues to grow and flourish because it has stayed true to its initial mission, which is to celebrate the lives of children with Down syndrome and to see them for the abilities, and not their disabilities.

## *Brighter Tomorrows*

As DSACK grew and the advocacy programs developed, we started hearing concerns from expectant parents and parents of newborns diagnosed with Down syndrome. These concerns centered on several issues.

First, some physicians' attitudes and perceptions of people with Down syndrome were extremely off base. Their "bedside manners" were, to say the least, a bit lacking. For example, we had a family whose child went undiagnosed six months, and when the diagnosis was finally made, the doctor took the view of, "Oh, no big deal, there's nothing you could have done it anyway."

Second, when a diagnosis is made, many treating physicians had no resource materials to provide to the patient. The doctors were giving them a very basic explanation of Down syndrome. Patients were being told to go to the Internet and do some research on their own. Many didn't even know of a local support group which they could reference or call for help, guidance and support.

What must patients be thinking at this point? They've got to be shell-shocked and feeling helpless. When you coupled these two issues, there was a major problem that needed to be solved. We were hearing this on a regular basis in our little part of the world. We magnified this across the country and quickly determined these were major concerns that needed some attention.

Harold and his colleagues at HDI and DSACK teamed together to build a training program for physicians that centered on Down syndrome education. With financial help from a Center for Disease Control grant, we were able to develop the Brighter Tomorrows training program.

The initial intent of Brighter Tomorrows was to educate physicians. The primary education was not from a diagnosis standpoint, but from a patient and community health standpoint. You see, a doctor's responsibility does not end with just a simple diagnosis. He or she has an obligation and a duty to ensure the best overall health and wellness of the patient, family and community.

What do I mean? Let me give you some real life examples.

**Example 1:**

A doctor delivers a newborn and quickly supplies the diagnosis that the baby has Down syndrome. He simply delivers the news and releases the baby to the parents. The only explanations and discussions surround the few facts about Down syndrome such as intellectual delays, potential hearing and eyesight issues, gastrointestinal issues, heart issues, physical delays, and on and on.

There is no discussion or informational exchange in regards to the support groups, points of access to resources such as literature, books, websites, therapy programs, financial resources and the like. There is no discussion as to the endless possibilities of a person with Down syndrome. There is no warmth and love for the patient or the family. It is simply a delivered message of the medical diagnosis. The family is stunned and traumatized, left to try and figure it out themselves.

Some figure it out, but many do not. We have seen several cases in which a child with Down syndrome is several years old and has never received any type of therapy. Why? Because the family was not aware of resources such as Kentucky's First Steps, where all of your therapies are covered by a state supported system.

**Example 2:**

An expectant mother decides to have prenatal testing and is told that her baby has Down syndrome. As in the first example, the only information given surrounds the intellectual and physical delays, and the potential medical issues such as hearing and eyesight deficiencies, and heart and gastrointestinal problems.

Again, the patient is never given information as to the opportunities and abilities of someone with Down syndrome. There is no unbiased, clinical-based information available for the patient, nor are they given information on where they can receive additional resources. Once again, they are left to make decisions on their own.

In this case, life-and-death decisions are made, as parents are given the choice of abortion, which many choose. This is extremely sad in my opinion, because the decision is made without all of the information at hand. The parents are not told how many people actually want to adopt a child with Down syndrome.

The parents are never exposed to the endless possibilities and opportunities for people with Down syndrome. They've never witnessed the transformational changes a child with special needs can have on a family and community. And finally, they do not realize that ending the life of an individual goes against the moral and ethical fiber of their very basic instinct and once this decision is made, it can never, ever be reversed. They do not realize the emotional trauma and heartbreak that will follow.

There is no blame to be cast here. The news of having a baby with a disability can be devastatingly emotional. Without accurate information decisions are made that most times are painfully regretted.

There are people who speak either outright or through public policy about preventing such disabilities as Down syndrome. These voices are most often heard through the auspices promoting prenatal testing specifically for Down syndrome.

There is great debate surrounding these tests and the reasoning and usefulness of them. I, for one, can only conclude that first, you will never prevent Down syndrome, and second, why would you want to do so? As the father of a child with Down syndrome, these tests, and the often resulting decision—abortion—greatly concern me.

The mere fact that we advocate the ending of a life because of a genetic difference is quite troubling. This is a very dangerous area to tread in my view. Will we start testing for hair color, sex, etc., and make decisions based on those genetic attributes? We already do, and I am deeply concerned with the innocent loss of another life, but I am equally or more concerned about the innocent loss of an entire family.

So, you may still ask, how does all this affect the health and wellness of a society and community? Well, let's look at the first example. When a child needs medical care and doesn't receive it, how does that affect the community? Most people think of this in terms of a physical illness such as the flu or the common cold. It's easy to see how this could affect the overall wellness of the community. Germs are spread, viruses are passed on and others get sick.

But not receiving necessary therapy and care? How does this impact the community? Let me share. What have we done if we do not train, educate and provide the necessary therapies to prepare our children to be productive members of society?

Productive members of society. Isn't that a pipe dream? Not at all. You don't have to look far to see people with Down syndrome working in your local businesses and markets. You don't have to look hard to find people with Down syndrome taking on more prominent roles as well. Karen Gaffney, who swam the English Channel as part of a relay team, is a self-advocate through her foundation, The Karen Gaffney Foundation. You have actor Chris Burke, who starred in the hit television series, "Life Goes On," and was nominated for a Golden Globe Award.

I would submit that we have failed. Not just failed the individual with special needs, but everyone. The lack of preventive intervention results in higher healthcare costs, which are avoidable. Early intervention and education provides the knowledge and resources to better understand the diagnosis and what we as parents and guardians need to know to provide proper care. This affects the entire community and society. Having a healthy and productive citizen promotes a healthy and productive community.

What about the second example? Let's take that out a bit further as well. Let's say a couple decides to terminate the pregnancy because they learn their baby has a disability. They make the decision under duress and without a full scope of knowledge, and soon feel in their hearts it was a big mistake. Guilt and remorse set in, and mental and emotional trauma ensue, negatively impacting an otherwise healthy marriage.

If they have other kids, they are invariable affected as well, along with all the other collateral damage that comes. Again, society and the community in a significant way are affected.

Now, there is the argument that terminating a pregnancy and not bringing a child with a disability into the world is healthy for the family and community. The argument goes something like this— the family doesn't have the burden and pain of having to raise a kid with a disability. Look at all the medical costs that are avoided.

The family can focus on raising their "normal" kids. The couple can always get pregnant again. And last but not least, marriage is already hard enough, so why add the extra pressure of having to raise a child with special needs?

I would submit to you the following.

- Burden and pain? Burden and pain are in the eye of the beholder. Yes, there are significant challenges, but the lessons, personal growth and knowledge that you and your child will experience greatly outweigh and overcome whatever burden and pain may come. The so-called burden and pain are only what you make it.
- Medical costs? Yes, there may be extra medical costs, but then again, there may not. Terminating the pregnancy guarantees extra medical costs. I'll take my chances on this one.
- Focus on the other kids? Having a child with special needs can actually help everyone focus on the family. It can bring everyone together to form a unique bond and identity.
- Divorce. A healthy marriage is something we all have to work on anyway. Marriage is a daily work in progress. That sounds trite, but so do most fundamentals. You will need a strong faith as this journey can't be handled alone.

The Brighter Tomorrows module has been used throughout the country in training and educating both practicing physicians and residents-in-training. It is accessed via the Web and a family version is now available in Spanish.

Shortly after we completed this module, (but to be honest, the idea came up during the production of it) we started the discussions of developing a module as a resource of information for parents and families. It just seemed that there were plenty of great resources out there, but something was lacking. No one could really put a finger on it.

We synthesized our thoughts down to one concept that best described this void in resources—it needed to be more personal. We needed to develop a resource that was personal. We felt this could best done by sharing our personal stories in a positive and celebratory way. We wanted to give people the opportunity to glimpse into our lives through pictorial stories and reflective narratives. We felt that if we put faces and personal stories together in this light of celebration, it could somehow ease their fears and trepidations.

So once again Harold and his research staff developed a most incredible Brighter Tomorrows module for families to personally see our stories. Pictures and reflective narratives allowed us to share our experiences and offer family glimpses.

A big reason for the success in advocating comes from understanding two realities. First, there is no perfect plan, solution or accommodation. Changes and adjustments can and will be made. Plans are not static. We all must be flexible and work with the plan that best accommodates all who are involved.

Second, budgets are limited. Our kids deserve the very best, no doubt, but we have to be mindful of the available resources. But, doesn't this go for everyone? Everyone who wants to be an attorney can't go to Harvard. We all have to learn to work with what's available. Our experience is that we have faced both of these realities, but we have learned to adapt and make suitable adjustments to assist Kate in maximizing her potential—and ours.

# SO, WHOSE EYES ARE YOU
# LOOKING THROUGH?

Ok, so we've spent some time getting to know me; now it's time to get to know you. For this,

I want to start off with some questions. The goal here is to help you get a baseline of your situation. Are you a parent, sibling, grandparent, aunt, uncle, cousin or friend, or just an avid reader without any experience with someone with special needs? Are you someone who received a false positive on a prenatal test and had to imagine raising a child with special needs?

I want you to get an understanding of where you are and how you feel about having a child with a disability. As I stated earlier, one of my goals is to alleviate the fear that you may have regarding a child with special needs. Whether your perspective is from a parent, a grandparent, a friend or some other relative of a child with special needs, take some time to answer these questions.

1. How would you react to your child being diagnosed with a disability such as Down syndrome? Would you be scared? Mad? Excited? Why and with whom would you be mad? Why would you react that way?
2. If you have a child with a disability, are you mad? Why and with whom are you mad? Are you bitter? Scared? Excited? Happy and overjoyed? Why do you feel the way you do?
3. If you found out prenatally, do you think your reaction would have been different if you would have found out at birth? Why or why not?

4.  How did family and friends react to the news? How should family and friends react? Now that's a tough one. Looking back, if you have a child with a disability, did people that you confided in give you good advice? Why or why not?

There are many reasons to feel the way you feel—you have that right. There is the unknown. Some of my insights and thoughts may make perfect sense and some may not. My quest is to get you thinking in a better light, through a different prism.

This is where the fun starts. The rest of the book will be dedicated to offering you the insights, retrospectives and reflections from my experiences of raising three wonderful daughters, the youngest with Down syndrome. I want to share with you the many joys that we have experienced.

Down syndrome in our family has brought many great memories and joyous occasions. It has provided many opportunities for personal growth and development that we otherwise would not have experienced. Beyond our wildest imaginations it has positively shaped and molded us as a family, neighborhood and community.

# SMALL MOMENTS THAT DEFINE

We are all given unique traits, personalities and characteristics. Coupling these with your daily actions, routines, and circumstances helps define who you are as a person. There are particular instances or events that turn out to be special defining moments that transcend all others. They are the ones that "stick in your brain" for all time. They become the short stories that we tell over and over again to friends and loved ones. The special defining moments that I speak are sometimes planned events, but many typically happen spontaneously and unexpectedly.

These defining moments started before Kate was even a week old. While still in the hospital, we decided to explain to Kala and Kelsey that Kate had Down syndrome, and exactly what that meant. Keep in mind that they were only eight and six at the time. As parents, we found it difficult to explain on a level that they could understand, so we enlisted the help of our pediatrician.

The pediatrician did a fantastic job of filtering down the diagnosis. She explained that Kate would need a little more extra love and assistance than most sisters, and she was really going to need their help. She said Kate was going to be like all sisters in that she was going to be annoying at times by getting into their stuff, playing with their toys and messing up their dolls. She discussed Down syndrome and what it was on a very basic level.

The defining moment came for us when Kala, who was eight at the time, said, "It doesn't matter what she has, and we're going to love her just the same." Through the eyes of an eight-year-old, we all were taught the very valuable lesson of unconditional love.

We all have been taught to have unconditional love for one another, but we as a family were experiencing it through our eight-year old daughter for her newborn sister. It was real; it was real life. It was being lived out by an eight-year-old girl who saw her baby sister as flawless while others were seeing her as something less than perfect.

We as a family learned in real time the meaning of unconditional love. We weren't just reading about it in some latest self-help book. We were living it right there in our family. If there was any doubt that we were going to treat Kate as anything less than perfect, it dissolved at that moment.

This unconditional love has spread to her friends as well. While Kate has completed her sixth and final year in elementary school, her friends became very special to her and she became special to them. Kate's teachers and principal have done an outstanding job of creating a culture of unconditional love for each other.

Each year we have our Buddy Walk fundraiser for DSACK. Many of Kate's teachers and friends regularly join in and support her.

This past year was exceptionally special. A young boy, Carson, showed up to walk with Kate. Carson's father told me that Carson had had a sleepover that night with his buddies and had a football game to play that day. Carson and his friends decided to miss playing their game to come walk and celebrate with Kate.

This type of friendship doesn't just happen. It is developed through guidance and teaching by family and community. Through a simply act of kindness, a young 11-year-old boy taught a life lesson to so many by opening up his heart and seeing the real Kate.

Taken individually, these small acts of kindness may not seem like much, but when they are part of who you are, when they come from your heart, they tell the world who you really are—they define you.

The defining moments come and go. Some are more noticeable than others. Special moments don't have to be major events that you'll remember, but instead, they can be common occurrences that provide special definition. Often my kids, out of blue as you would call it, will simply, in the most sincere way, lean over or look up and say, "Dad, I love you."

It tends to be so random, but when they say it, you can tell that they really mean it. You can tell that they really understand what love is and what makes it up. There's nothing better than getting one of these from your kids. These moments truly define where their heart is centered. It reassures me of how they feel about me, but more importantly, it defines who they are and what makes their heart beat.

It is so much fun to recognize these special moments. I suspect that as I age and grow bit wiser, I learn to appreciate them; I learn to keep a sharper eye out for them. When they occur, I file them back in my memory for safe-keeping.

I find myself searching for opportunities that will allow for these special moments to occur. It's a small thing, but fulfilling Kate's request for a snack at her favorite sandwich shop is a special occasion for her.

When we jump in the car, she loves to hook up her IPod and crank up the volume. Having a rolling disco club is a small thing, but she gets a real kick out of it, while I wonder if I need to head to the doctor to have my hearing checked.

It's a small thing, but when Kala and Kelsey were in grade school, we developed a tradition of stopping at Waffle House for breakfast. Today, I will spontaneously treat them to lunch and listen to their concerns or hear about their career aspirations. These special moments have enabled us to create a special bond and over the years have culminated in some special moments.

It's a small thing, but occasionally I will surprise Karen by giving her flowers for no reason. I usually do this when I'm in trouble, but it gives me an opportunity to show her my appreciation and to say, 'thank you,' for all she does for our family.

I do these things with heartfelt love. I do these things because I want to do them. All of these things, when taken individually, are no big deal, but when you combine them over the course of time, they become part of who you are; they become what defines you. I suspect that for most people, that definition starts at a young age, much like Kala and Carson.

# INFLUENCING OTHERS

We all would like to think we've made some positive influence on the people around us, and to be honest, most everyone has influenced and enriched others in their lives in a very positive and dramatic way. As I look back on my life, the people who have influenced me the most are not what I would call extraordinary people. They've been very simple people living very simple lives.

My grandfather was that way. He wasn't famous and didn't have a lot of money. I remember a very simple man, working as an off-shore oil driller and driving a truck for a local oil and gas distributor in south Louisiana. I remember a man who was committed to his wife and remained that way for over 60 years. I remember a man who never missed Sunday mass and was an active member in the Knights of Columbus, a man who honored God and loved his family, and was committed to earning an honest day's pay.

My grandfather taught me, not by his words, but by his actions. He taught me that keeping your priorities in order—faith, family and work—was the key to winning the long race of life.

Kate has already had such a positive influence on so many people, and she's not even a teenager yet. It has been a blessing to see. Some of these influences have been small and heart-warming, while others have determined career choices.

Kate had just turned one when we first moved to Lexington. The state of Kentucky has an excellent early intervention program for children with special needs. One of the therapists had a daughter who was just graduating from high school and was looking for babysitting opportunities. With no family in the area, we quickly summoned for her services.

Meaghan and Kate developed a bond and friendship that was special. She loved Kate and that love was reciprocated. Meaghan soon moved off to college, but we stayed in touch with her mother. A couple of years later, I was talking with her mom and I asked how her daughter was doing. She said Meaghan was doing great and told me that she had decided to major in special education because of her experiences with Kate.

Kate had the same influence on Kelsey, her older sister. Kelsey decided she wanted to be a pediatric physical therapist upon graduating from high school. She recalls how much of a difference it made for Kate with having the therapist at such an early age.

Kelsey knows the bonds that Kate has made over the years through the different therapy programs. She sees the satisfaction the therapists get from helping a young child grow and develop skills that will enable them to achieve their life goals.

In the summer of 2010, Karen and Kate had the pleasure of meeting a Japanese national student. As part of a class, she was asked to spend some time with a family that had a member with a disability. She was put in contact with us and spent a couple of days getting to know Karen and Kate.

Their first meeting was for lunch at our neighborhood pool, where she got to observe Kate swimming and interacting with her friends. Speaking in broken English, the student shared her background and experiences with Karen and Kate. Karen shared with her some intimate reflections about our experiences and how we love Kate and wouldn't want her any other way.

Karen said the short meeting brought tears of joy as they were both able to gain greater insight into life and a renewed strength to see things in a more positive perspective. Karen shared with me how spiritual the meeting was to her. Both were graced by new understandings as well as new questions.

Why were two people from completely opposite ends of the earth brought together in such a small and peaceful part of the world? How did two people from such different backgrounds have such similar spirits? Why was there such an immediate spiritual bond between Kate and the student? Karen told me that there was something special about this student but she just couldn't put her finger on it. She hoped that each would keep in touch through their journeys in life.

Karen and Kate recently received a letter from her that I would like to share like to share.

*Dear Karen,*

*I hope you, Kate and other family members are doing well. I am sorry that I have not contacted you for soooo long time. I have been thinking of you and Kate often in my mind but this academic year has been truly overwhelming. I've had a very tough time but so far have been surviving☺ I'm truly glad about it. I truly appreciate that you kindly listened to me when I suddenly called you and cried last summer. That was so strange, wasn't it? I'm sorry about it. I felt so lonely at that time, and at that time, I had some very difficult issues. Things have been much better now, or I can say that I may be used to dealing with the situation. Anyway, the time that I called you was the hardest time. Thank you again for listening, understanding, and encouraging me.*

*By the way, as I said on the phone, I bought a T-shirt for Kate in Japan last summer. I can't believe that I didn't give it to her until now! Sorry! I hope this size of the T-shirt is still fine for her.*

*You and Kate are always shining in my heart. It was one of the best encounters since I came to the U.S. You and Kate gave me a lot of important treasures. My daily life is just busy, busy, and busy, nothing special, but I'm always keeping something very important which I can't tell in words deep in my heart. I can't explain what it is, but it's something that I can connect with you, Kate and other people who have the same spirits.*

*I hope you have a great spring!*

*Please say, "Hi!" to Kate for me☺*

*How is she doing?*

Wow! I never thought a young girl and her mother could have such a powerful impact on an individual's heart and soul without really even trying. Here is a person who was pulling strength from her relationship with Kate to get through what she felt was the hardest time in her life.

This is true testimony that we all can have a great influence on those we come in contact with each and every day. Sometimes we realize it, but most times we don't. Sometimes it is a concerted effort to try and influence, but most times it's not.

Most times, our influence on others is just how we live our daily lives. Our influence is just us as ordinary people doing ordinary things, but doing them exceptionally well. What started out as just a simple class project turned into a life-altering experience for everyone. Why was this possible? Because of Kate, living just an ordinary life, but doing it very well.

These are just a few examples as to how Kate has made a profound difference in people's lives, and she's only 12 years old. How many other times has Kate made a difference in someone's life without us even knowing about it? But doesn't that go for everyone? None of us really know what kind of influence we have on others.

The fact that you have made a positive influence on another is the greatest compliment you can receive. My challenge to you is to quietly influence others through simple, everyday actions. Kate did it just by attending therapy sessions with a bright and cheery attitude, and meeting someone through their college curriculum.

# ADAPTING TO A WAY OF LIFE

I'm always amazed at the adaptive skills of all living creatures. The process for some things has taken literally millions of years. It could be webbed feet on a duck or large lung capacity for a whale. The process can also be much quicker, such as adapting to a quick change in temperature as we do in cold or hot climates.

Many people think the ability to adapt is the one human characteristic or trait that greatly determines one's success, and in many cases, one's success to literally survive. Having to change the way you have been doing something for many years can not only seem to be very difficult, it can be very difficult.

What I find very interesting is how people with disabilities learn to adapt. We see this on a regular basis in people who lose a limb, or their eyesight or hearing. Years of hard work and assistance from therapists are needed to adapt to the change. We see it regularly with people who are also born with a disability. Again, it could be someone who is deaf or blind. It could also be someone who has Down syndrome or Autism, or any other intellectual or physical disability.

When I was an undergraduate in college, I crossed paths with one particular individual who was totally blind. It was amazing to see him function and maneuver around campus. He walked everywhere and never seemed to make a wrong turn, always arriving at his destination.

One distinctive thing I remember is seeing him at the recreation center. He enjoyed swimming and jumping off the diving board—not just cannonballs, but actually diving! He would come into the natatorium, find his way to the diving board and climb up the ladder, all without assistance. Once on the board, he would use his toes to find the edges and the end of the board. He would then take two bounces and dive. He would surface, swim to the edge of the pool and go again. To this day, I find what I witnessed simply amazing.

What we, from the outside looking in, see as an obstacle, is not an obstacle at all for those who see it from the inside looking out. They have learned to adapt to the situation and they've adapted to it as if it was never a problem. It's their way of life.

Now, I'm sure that if we could offer a blind man sight or a deaf man the ability to hear, we would certainly do that, and I am confident that they would certainly oblige. But knowing that this isn't possible they accept their circumstances and adapt to them—and they do it without complaint or misgiving, which is quite amazing in my mind.

I bring this up because many times we find ourselves wishing we could change a situation or, more specifically to our discussion here, a diagnosis. We need to be very careful about these wishes. If we change one thing, what other things must change as a result? What opportunities, learning and growth experiences will be missed? An entire life path would be redirected. It could be good, but it could also be bad.

Several years ago I met a gentleman named Charles. On our first encounter, I had a very nice visit with him. My family and I had just moved to Lexington and I was making a sales call to Charles' law office in the small town of Winchester, Kentucky. I noticed he had a picture of his son, Matthew, who happens to have Down syndrome, on his desk. Matthew had just graduated from high school and was starting a new chapter in his life. We had a very nice chat as we shared our common bond of having children with Down syndrome.

We laughed as Charles recalled some of the most memorable experiences he'd had with Matthew over the years. Our visit turned most interesting as we wondered aloud what we'd do if our kids did not have Down syndrome. What if we could somehow, magically, make Down syndrome go away?

Now, keep in mind that I was still relatively new to the scene in regards to being the parent of a child with a disability, so I wasn't quite sure where my heart stood on this issue.

Charles, however, was a seasoned veteran in this arena, and had a bit more wisdom. He said, unequivocally, that if a doctor were to ever find a pill that would make Down syndrome go away, he wouldn't want Matthew to take it. "Wow!," I thought." I didn't ask him why, but I did spend a lot of time pondering his point of view. After some time had passed and I gained more perspective as a parent, his viewpoint began to make more sense.

You see, Matthew is his own person. His family and friends know him no differently. They wouldn't want him any other way. Matthew certainly knows no difference.

Matthew had learned to adapt to his circumstances just like we all learn to adapt to our own. So many things would change if Matthew changed. There are so many family memories that just simply would not be there if Matthew was any different.

I don't know if Matthew himself would want anything to change. At first thought I suppose he would, as many things would be easier, less trouble and a bit more convenient.

I suppose we all think that changing something about ourselves would make life much easier; I know I do. I often think, if I had a higher IQ, or if I were a bit taller or shorter, somewhere, somehow, I could have been better at something, or things would have come a bit easier. Well, I can't change who I am. I can only work to get better and improve my current self; I can't change my core genetic makeup.

As for Matthew, I guarantee the love people have for him and the compassion his family and friends show him would not be stronger if he were different. His family loves him unconditionally. They love him for who he is and not for what he can or can't do. That my friends, when it's all said and done, is what life's all about.

# YOU ARE WHO YOU ARE

I feel the same way about Kate as Matthew's father did about him. Kate is Kate. I wouldn't want her any other way. That's the feeling I have about all my kids; each is special in their own way.

I couldn't imagine my oldest daughter being taller just so she could be a better basketball player, or my middle daughter being shorter so she could be a better cheerleader. The same is true for Kate, because she has so much to offer. Kate has tremendous opportunities to change and shape this world for the better.

Kate is already a fantastic leader and change agent for others. She is teaching and influencing where no one else can. Why would we want to change that? Because *we* think it would be easier for her?

Let's pause for a moment so I can explain an important point here. I'm not saying that I wouldn't change some of the symptoms or behaviors that come with Down syndrome, especially if they endanger her or others. For example, many kids with Down syndrome or Autism experience attention deficit disorder. This can potentially be very dangerous for them, as well as extremely detrimental in their learning and education process.

There's medication to help them focus, thus improving their safety and learning ability. This is a symptom of the disability. It's not the disability or their genetic makeup. I'm always willing to provide medicine to offset symptoms. We are always looking for ways to improve the lives of people with disabilities. There's great research in the areas of therapies and medicines that can greatly enhance their lives, and we want to continue those advancements.

What I struggle with is the interest in reversing or "undoing" what genetically makes up a person at his/her core. When you do this, you begin to change the soul of that person. You begin to change the very foundation, the very beginning of that person. Changing the soul and foundation of someone creates and changes so much more. It completely changes that person. We all have flaws, but I don't think we want someone to genetically change our core makeup.

I often think of all the things that Kate will not get to experience because of her disability, and it's easy to get depressed and saddened. On the flip side however, if you chart all of the things that she can do and will be able to do in spite of her disability it's quite amazing.

Several years ago, a photo of our three daughters was taken to a local artist so he could draw a portrait of them. The artist did a wonderful job; however he didn't quite get Kate. What he had trouble with was drawing the unique features that come with Down syndrome, like the beautiful, almond-shaped eyes and the broad lips.

The finished portrait, however, was quite intriguing to me. What resulted was a rendering of Kate without Down syndrome. The picture is no doubt beautiful, but when I look at the picture I don't quite see the real Kate. I don't see the uniqueness of her.

I don't see Kate's innocence, her warm heart, or her hugs and kisses as we meet each other after a long day apart. I don't see the lessons that Kate teaches to everyone she meets. I don't see the bright future that Kate has ahead of her. In short, I see a different child, a different Kate, and when I see a different Kate, I see a different family.

Kate helps define our family. We are who we are because each one of us brings our own uniqueness. Kate, like each of us, helps define our family. Changing her changes everything.

Why would you want to alter Kate's uniqueness? Because you think it would ease a few burdens? I submit to you that it may ease some burdens, but others would arise as a result. Love and accept what has been given. It is a gift beyond your imagination. Nurture it, tend to it like the delicate flower that it is and allow it to grow. Develop it and allow it to be the change agent that it's so capable of being.

# EXPECTATIONS

I often find myself totally forgetting that Kate has a disability; a strange thought I suppose, given the fact that she has several unique physical features. At times, I find myself expecting her to do the same things that my other kids do. I often find myself expecting her to perform like the typical kids her age. This recently led me to ask a simple question—should I have different expectations for Kate because she has a disability?

I think the answer here is both yes and no. Yes, we do need to have different expectations in terms of her capabilities, but no, I don't think we should have different expectations in terms of her working and performing to the best of her abilities.

It would be wrong to expect her to be a rocket scientist or a brain surgeon . . . she simply doesn't have the intellectual capacity (IQ). It would be wrong to expect her to be a world-class runner because she just doesn't have the physical capabilities.

However, if we determine that she can read and comprehend on, say, a sixth grade level, then we should expect her to meet that challenge. If she has the strength and agility to ride a bike, then we should expect her to learn how to ride a bike. What we have to do is establish what her capabilities are and then expect her to be the best that she can be, given those capabilities.

Kate has to be accountable and responsible for her actions and behaviors in the realm of what her abilities are at the time and what she is capable of doing. This is the foundation for her learning both social skills and intellectual skills (reading, writing and arithmetic). We are constantly evaluating, not only amongst ourselves, but with her educators; what is she capable of doing and what is her ability level at that particular point in time.

One of the mistakes I think some parents and guardians make is putting too much emphasis and pressure on their special needs child—or on their typical child, for that matter—to perform at a certain level. For us as parents and guardians of special needs children, we have to accept that our children will most likely not ever perform at the same level as a typical child. That just isn't going to happen for the majority of those with an intellectual disability and developmental delay.

We recently met with a behavioral researcher and she put this in excellent perspective. Kate was transitioning from elementary school to middle school and we were discussing the fact that she was reading at a second-grade level. We were reviewing some plans to address her reading comprehension when I made the comment that our goal and expectation was to get her to be able to read at "grade level" by the time she was entering high school. The researcher quickly stopped me and said that was unrealistic. She said Kate may one day be able to read at her age appropriate level, but it's going to take her a bit longer. She said a much more realistic short term goal would be to get her to at least read on a sixth-grade level.

Why? First, from her evaluation, Kate has the capability to accomplish this objective. Second, at sixth-grade level, people have the ability to read and comprehend most anything. A little-known fact is that newspapers, magazines and most periodicals are written on a sixth-grade level.

The researcher said our goal should be to get Kate to a reading level which would allow her to read these types of publications. By accomplishing this, she would, at the very minimum, enjoy reading and be able to "function" on her own. That meant our goal should be to get her to at least a sixth-grade level, then revise and evaluate her goals and expectations as she progresses.

By educating ourselves and knowing Kate's capabilities and abilities, we're able to better teach her. How difficult would it be for all of us if we did not have this knowledge and understanding? Nothing is more frustrating than being unaware of your child's abilities and what that child is capable of doing. Can you imagine the frustration for both the student and their teacher if they are trying to learn algebra when the student doesn't have the ability to learn it yet?

Once you have clarified your child's abilities and capabilities, whether or not they have a disability, the learning and educating goes much smoother. Once again, it's an ever-changing process and there is constant evaluation. It occurs both in the formal learning process (school) and in everyday experiences and situations.

This is a much easier process with a typical child versus one with a disability, such as Down syndrome, Autism, etc. Most of us— parents, educators and medical professionals—are keenly aware of the expected abilities and capabilities of a typical child. There is not much variance if there is no disability involved. However for a child with a disability, more is required.

Each child is quite different in terms of their abilities and capabilities. You know your child the best, but outside assistance can certainly help. We have been very blessed to have met and worked with some of the best educators and medical professionals. Kate has been evaluated so we can all learn where she is and what she can become. This is an on-going process. It is never static as she grows and develops every day.

I think it's perfectly acceptable to have expectations for Kate just as I do for my other kids. Like all of us, if she feels no accountability, if she has no sense of expectation to work and behave within her capacity as a young, productive and orderly individual, then the core bedrock needed to be successful is eroded.

Without holding Kate accountable and without having clear expectations for her, we would be undermining her ability to understand that there are certain responsibilities for her. Completing homework, attending dance practice and being an integral part of the family through chores are all responsibilities for which Kate knows she is accountable. These responsibilities teach Kate to grow and mature, just like they do for any child. When this is missing, our ultimate goal for her of becoming a productive citizen in society is lost.

Keeping in mind that Kate has a disability is sometimes difficult for me when it comes to making sure her responsibilities are completed. Remembering that she may require additional time or different instructions is often forgotten. A bit more time to get ready for school or a lot more guidance for homework is often needed, but many times dismissed. She knows that homework, getting ready for school or going to bed on time is required.

This is where I have to keep in mind her capacity and abilities, and my expectations need to be adjusted. We just can't turn off the TV, give her instructions and expect her to do it right away. She needs a bit more guidance and assistance. I forget that detail many times when I give her a task or chore to complete. I get busy with my own work and 30 minutes later, she's off and onto something else that's more appealing. Frustration towards her sinks in, but the frustration should be at me and not at her. I have to remember that she has Down syndrome and it requires a bit more one-on-one attention to keep her on task.

One troubling thought I had when Kate was a newborn was her level of functioning. I wondered what I could expect her to be able to do. Wanting some type of peek into her future, I asked that very question to a group of her in-home therapists. Their response was inspiring and gave me a whole new perspective on how I would approach not only Kate, but each of my kids. They simply said no one really knows her ability, or any other person's ability, for that matter. Yes, through evaluations and observances we can come close to measuring one's capability, but no one really knows for sure.

From then on, we have not put limits on what Kate can do. At the same time, we are constantly re-evaluating our expectations and goals for her. The one foundational component that we use to set these goals and expectations is this—what skill sets does/will she need to maximize her *enjoyment of life*? Now "enjoy life" could mean different things to different people, but I think it comes back to the core concept I have been discussing here in that someone will more fully enjoy life if he/she is living up to their potential and capabilities.

We are continually monitoring her progress, evaluating her abilities, and adjusting our goals and our expectations of her, in all phases of her life—from school and extracurricular activities to her spiritual life and social life. Once again, what I have found is that this same approach is the one that I have implemented with each of our kids . . . and it's working . . . I think!

# WHAT I SEE

Kate, as with all people, has been blessed with many talents and abilities. She loves to ride her bike, swim, jump on her trampoline and play on her swing set. Kate doesn't want to be treated any differently because of her disability, and we try to comply with her wishes. If her abilities allow, she participates in normal extracurricular activities such as company dances, piano lessons, choir, swimming, and the bowling team. There are things, however, that we simply can't avoid modifying, such as her education plan, providing therapy sessions, etc. When her ability doesn't allow these normal activities, she participates in the modified sports programs such as Special Olympics Cheerleading.

Many people may wonder and sometimes ask, what do you see when you look at your daughter who has a disability? Do you see her any differently than your other kids? These are simple questions that should invoke some simple answers, right? Well, here's my short and simple answer.

I don't see Kate's disabilities at all. I see all of her abilities, just like I see the abilities of our other kids. I see all that she can do and wants to do, and we do whatever we can to assist her in accomplishing her dreams and ambitions, just like our other kids.

I see a young girl with beautiful blue eyes and mid-length auburn hair, standing tall for her age and of medium build, and experiencing her adolescent, awkward growth spurt. I see a young girl looking forward to her next orthodontist appointment so she can change the color on her braces while at the same time marking off the days until she can rid herself of the annoying wires and bands in order to show off her new, beautiful smile.

I see a girl growing so fast that we can't update her wardrobe quick enough to keep up with her ever-changing fashion requirements. Gone are the days of shopping in the pre-teen department; it's on to the junior miss section where the prices seem to double and the designs are, might I say, a bit more revealing.

I see a girl experiencing the joys as well as the trials and tribulations of trying to develop her social network of friends and social life. Her classmates and friends have been wonderful in welcoming her into their group, but like all young teenagers, she sometimes feels a bit left out and a bit unwanted, just like my other kids did at that age.

I see a young girl wanting to grow up faster than she is able to at this time. In other words, she's 13 but thinks she's 23. Kate loves the latest Top 40 songs in pop/rock and country. Upon her learning of her favorite music act coming to town, somehow she finds a way to convince us to attend. She's at the age where being seen with her parents is not cool but she's not old enough to be left unattended, which is quite the challenge for this still adolescent girl, the same way it was for my other kids.

I see a young girl who learns what she wants to learn and complains when she has to participate in the homework task that are boring and mundane to her. She figured out how to operate the VCR/DVD player at a very young age. She's loaded her IPod and IPad with her playlist and has ITunes on 'speed dial.'

She somehow figured out my Apple ID password and knows how to place an order and/or download the latest 'app.' I never knew Kate would breach my security measures. She knows how to navigate movies and shows via, "On Demand" and, like most, could watch them all night long. She can get your virtual interactive games set up and will then proceed to beat you at virtual bowling, tennis and dancing.

I see a girl who loves her family more than anything in the world. She has a special place in her heart for each of her sisters as well as her mom, dad, aunts, uncles, cousins and grandparents. She wakes up with a hug for each and reminds us of bedtime prayers before we rest our heads on the pillow at night.

I see a girl that loves it when she gets to hang out with her current friends and meet new ones. It's not just meeting new friends but its developing friendships with them.

We recently joined the summer adult/youth bowling league and the kids in the league have been so kind to Kate with their bowling tips and encouragement. They truly like having Kate in their group and Kate loves her new-found friendships.

I see a girl who is the first to say, "Bless You," when someone sneezes. If you have a string of seven sneezes, as I often do, you'll get a string of seven, "Bless You's," from Kate (most stop the Bless You's at three). I see a girl who always asks how the sick and infirmed are doing and prays for them to get better. I see a girl who mourns the loss of a loved one and prays for them to watch over us.

I see a girl who enjoys going to church and participating in the Mass. I see a young girl developing her spiritual life and her relationship with her God. Church service is a weekly gathering for her and she so much looks forward to it. I see a strong-willed girl who enjoys and revels in her accomplishments and achievements. Whether it's learning to tie her shoes, riding her bike for the first time, bowling a strike, winning a card or board game, or graduating from elementary school, she gets so excited and beams with joy and confidence. Nothing makes a parent more proud than to see their children achieve their goals, no matter how big or small.

I see a girl who gets a sassy mouth with her parents when she's told not do something or that she can't do something she wants to do. I see a girl who's learned a few "adult" words along the way and sometimes can't seem to keep from repeating them. I see an adolescent who can be defiant when she doesn't get her way.

I see all of these things in Kate just as I do in her sisters and in most other young girls making their way to adulthood. Kate's growing up, blazing her own trail, living her own life and touching people in her own amazing way. She is no different, in these regards, than our other daughters.

Kate has a very outgoing personality. I would definitely say she's a people person. Many people say the acorn didn't fall far from the tree on this one as her mother seems to never meet a stranger. Kate always has a handshake, a hug or a nice word for everyone she meets.

A few years ago, when Kate was about nine or 10 years old, her teacher was working with her on manners as part of her lesson plan. One lesson focused on how to greet people. Her teacher explained to Kate that proper etiquette called for a handshake and a cordial greeting such as, "Hello," or, "How are you."

Well, one of Kate's favorite teachers, a man, came walking down the hall—it was time for Kate to get in some practice. As he approached, Kate's teacher greeted him and then it was Kate's turn. Kate shook his hand and said, "Hello." Kate's teacher prompted her to say something nice and complimentary and Kate responded by telling him, "Hey, you're hot!" Needless to say, there were a couple of red faces; but there was a young girl who got a charge out of making everyone laugh.

That same year, soon after this, the new superintendent of schools visited Kate's elementary class. As he was introducing himself, Kate stood up, walked over to him, held out her hand and said, "Hi, my name is Kate Boudreaux, very nice to meet you." The new superintendent was very impressed with Kate's manners and outgoing personality. While the other students were the normal shy fifth graders, Kate had no fears. Her outgoing personality was certainly on display and everyone enjoyed her genuine kindness.

As I mentioned in the prior chapter, we have the same expectation for Kate just as we do for our other children, and that is to perform to the level of your ability and talents—nothing more, nothing less—and to use those talents to make the world a better place.

We are all given certain abilities and talents. Some of us have extremely high I.Q.'s, while some of us are athletically gifted. Whatever the case, it is our responsibility as parents to nurture these talents, both in ourselves and in our kids. If we don't, we have failed ourselves and our kids.

It's always very interesting to see how kids migrate to the activities and associations that suit their interest and abilities. Some enjoy sports and some enjoy the arts, while others find science and math entertaining and rewarding. They use these avenues to develop themselves and to give them an opportunity grow and mature.

I, as a parent, see these activities and associations as opportunities to grow and develop relationships with others and to create lasting memories; ones that you may lean on simply to cherish for old time's sake or ones that you keep in your learning bank to use for future advice.

We recently attended the largest cheerleading competition in Atlanta with Kate as she was on the Special Olympics cheerleading squad here in Lexington. There were so many wonderful things about the trip. Kate's sister, Kelsey, was able to make the trip, and as a former cheerleader herself it was fun for her to be able watch her kid sister perform. Karen's mother, Nana, was able to go as well, so Kate had quite a personal entourage.

Kate's teammate and good friend, 23-year-old Megan, who has Down syndrome, rode with us as her parent's needed to stay home to work. Megan is an amazing individual; she's an accomplished pianist, an excellent cheerleader (she can complete over six consecutive back handsprings), has her driver's permit and recently graduated from college with an associate's degree.

Our trip first took us to Nashville for an overnight stay to pick up Nana as she there visiting with Karen's brother.

The trip started in typical fashion, with me getting mad because of our late departure and the fact that not all the luggage would fit. Kate and Megan had their electronic devices loaded with their playlists and headphones in place. Karen was the designated pilot and Kelsey her faithful navigator, while I was relegated to the third row seat.

All went well for 15 minutes, then came the first 'pee' break. All was well for another 30 minutes, then the, "I'm hungry," chorus began. I would have been upset, but hey, I wasn't driving! We finally made it to Nashville in record time (record for taking the longest).

We visited with my brother-in-law and his family at their new house, and had a nice dinner before bunking down for the night at a hotel in preparation for the next day's long drive. As we were eating, unbeknownst to the rest of us, Megan slips out of the dining room and into the living room, where the baby grand piano resides.

She proceeds to play, Beethoven's "Fur Elise"—no sheet music, straight from memory. We all just stopped what we were doing and quizzically looked at each other as if to ask if she was really playing the piano, and if so, was she really playing that score. It was very moving to say the least and it was one small act that really made our trip special.

We made our way to the hotel where Kate and Megan got their own room with Kelsey. It's not a big deal to you or I when we get our own room, but it certainly is for teenagers. Kate thought she wasn't 13, but 23. It was the little things such as these that made the entire weekend special and well worth the time. Kate and her team finished second out of 13 teams, and they are already preparing for next year's season.

Kate loves the performing arts. Her piano lessons, dance and choir allow her to express herself, as well as give her additional ways to grow, mature and learn. It's her dream to one day be in a live theatrical production. She is a natural actress who's always looking for a part. Unlike her parents, she doesn't suffer from severe stage fright. I'm certain, that with her determination and passion, she will one day accomplish this dream.

Kate enjoys school and school enjoys her. We've had a wonderful experience working with her teachers and school staff over the years. There was a period of time when Kate was not interested in school and, in particular, in doing her homework. Through careful observation by her family and her teachers, we identified some potential obstacles. We modified the work and when she started getting better results (which for her are smiley faces and A-plus marks) they excited and motivated her. Nothing excites a student more than getting a good report, and that includes Kate.

Much of our time and focus is naturally spent on helping our kids grow intellectually, which is as it should be. Education is a major determining factor in how productive we can be to society. One area that can greatly affect our intellectual progress and educational experience is our social life. This holds true for our older daughters and for all kids. What I have found is when their social life isn't in harmony, it affects everything. When their social life is a train wreck, attitudes are depressed and this ultimately affects educational and extracurricular performances.

Kate is no different. She loves having friends and enjoys an active social life. Having a vibrant social life with an abundance of friends can be difficult for a child with an intellectual disability, especially through the adolescent years. The difficulty tends to arises simply out of the communication barrier. As kids begin to see and understand there is a developmental delay, they tend to avoid the kids with limited communication skills, especially if there's a lack of education regarding people with disabilities.

Conversely, kids with disabilities begin to realize the differences as well. They become aware of them, and thus a level of inferiority takes hold. The result is that they don't reach out to make the connections with friends. The overall result is that the kids don't develop critical relationships; relationships that can have a lifelong, profound difference in each ones' life.

DSACK and other organizations have done a tremendous job of putting together learning and awareness presentations for both parents and children. The presentations are interactive and explain some of the physical and intellectual challenges that come with not only Down syndrome but with other disabilities. Once a child has attended a presentation, you can immediately see the simple awareness factor increases their comfort level. In turn, you see an increase in the social interaction, which is where the relationships begin and friendships develop.

For Kate, her classmates and her teachers, it was a game changer. When Kate began the fifth grade, Karen shared with the class a presentation on Down syndrome. Keep in mind that very few of Kate's classmates, friends or teachers had any experience with Down syndrome.

The kids were able to learn what Down syndrome is and how it affects you. It gave them a brief glimpse of the world through the eyes of someone with Down syndrome.

Since that time, Kate's peers have taken a special interest in her. She had two girls in her class volunteer to help tutor her. Kids began helping her a bit more on the playground and were more sensitive to make sure she was included. They taught her how to jump rope along with how to play basketball and volleyball.

Kate's teacher was able to better understand how she learns and how she can enhance the overall learning experience in the classroom. It was wonderful to see how everyone benefitted through these transformative behaviors.

We recently asked Kate's teacher to assist us in the second phase of the Brighter Tomorrows project with a reflection of Kate and here is what she shared.

*As a teacher for 22 years, I had never had a student with Down syndrome in my classroom, so to say I was completely comfortable and felt like I knew exactly what to do the day Kate walked through the door wouldn't be completely honest. What I realized early into the year, was I didn't need to worry about a thing; Kate would teach me.*

*Several of my students had been with Kate the previous year, but some of her very best friends this year were new to her. For example, two girls in my classroom were happy to step up and help Kate with math facts in the mornings. The bottom line is, Kate was a friend to these children and so they embraced her as well.*

*Working with Kate and talking with her in free time helped me get to know her in a way that would allow me to plug into her interests and the things she enjoyed doing. Kate has truly taught me what I needed to know to teach her in both social and academic situations. In classes that were more difficult, we would find a way to engage her that was appropriate.*

*We sing and move a lot, work in small groups, and we use an interactive white board and computer to help her participate.*

*Kate was quick to let me know what she enjoyed and what she didn't and I filed it all away, remembering that for future lessons. The relationship we shared was the key to success in my classroom.*

*What a wonderful and memorable year I had with Kate! I will forever be changed by a family with an amazing outlook and confidence in their child to achieve, by a classroom of students embracing a young lady that just wants to be their friend, and most of all by a beautiful, joyful young person who constantly lets me know of her love for me and her zest for life.*

We've been blessed with many teachers over the years who have led to Kate's personal, social and classroom success.

As Kate transitioned to middle school, she blossomed with the further assistance of her wonderful new teachers, assistants and friends. One of the extracurricular clubs that Kate joined was the Gummy Bear Club. This group was formed to offer all kids, both typical and special needs, the opportunity to work together on community and school projects.

Their overall philosophy and motto is, "Seeing with your heart and not your eyes." Their main goal is to make sure all kids feel included and feel welcome at school and in society. The typical students act as peer tutors in many different areas such as homework assistance, social partnering and life skills training. It's amazing to see the participation.

I was surprised to hear that out of all the clubs at school, the Gummy Bear Club has the most members. Kate loves the club and we credit it with much of her success in transitioning to middle school.

One of Karen and mine's goals was to enable Kate to receive a Catholic, Christian education. We have always understood the inherent challenges and obstacles to accomplishing this; school funding and resources, but we've continued to hope that this dream would become reality one day. Karen and I have fond memories of our catholic education and we were fortunate enough to provide that same experience to Kala and Kelsey. We all value that experience and hold the relationships which were born from it very close to our hearts. It was from that experience that we so strongly wanted Kate to have the same opportunity.

For the past several years Karen has been on the Dioceses of Lexington's 'Inclusion Committee.' Their main purpose has been to develop a better understanding of what is needed within the catholic schools so that they to enable them to provide the learning resources for kids with special needs.

Slowly, the committee has made, and continues to make, tremendous progress toward their intended goal.

The local catholic high school now has a "High Marks" program. One of its purpose is to provide kids that may have learning challenges dedicated, specialized resources such as private study areas and tutors and specialized teaching aids and methods.

The president of Lexington's St. Peter and Paul regional catholic elementary and middle school, Jeanne Miller, is on the committee with Karen. Over the last few months, she has been working with her staff and administration on developing and implementing programs and resources needed to educated kids with learning differences.

With them in place for the 2013-14 school year, Jeanne and her staff felt they were ready to serve kids with special needs the quality Catholic education which they offer to all others. Jeanne invited us to visit the school with the hope that we would give Kate the opportunity to attend.

This decision wasn't to be taken lightly. We were pleased with where she was going to school, but we understood the importance of the Christian setting. We knew Kate would be the first child with special needs to attend St. Peter and Paul. We weren't naïve to the fact that when you are the first, the trail blazer, the pioneer, it is inherent that you will experience a lot of unforeseen challenges and obstacles. Was Kate ready to move to her second school in a year? Were we as a family, and was the school and the Catholic education community, prepared to accept the opportunity?

After consulting with Jean and her staff and a careful assessment of Kate's abilities, and a lot of prayerful thought, we made the decision to give Kate the opportunity to attend St. Peter and Paul.

The experience has been nothing short of a blessing for Kate. The faculty and staff have opened not only their minds, but most importantly, their hearts, to her. Many teachers take their "free period" and work with Kate as needed, such being her scribe during a class or as a tutor during the school day.

But it's not just staff; it's not just the teachers; it's the students as well. They have welcomed Kate into their school and lives. Like most experiences, it's the little things that have made the biggest impact. Little things, like Kate never having to worry about eating lunch alone as someone always invites her to eat with them. In Kate's guitar class, one of Kate's new friends, without being asked, sits with Kate and helps her learn how to play. We all know it is working when, shortly after Kate was in school, a parent of one of her friends told Karen that her daughter, in her night time prayer vigil, prayed that Kate would enjoy her new school and that she would like it. All of this is evidence that we have made the right choice. Learning doesn't just come from the textbook.

We constantly work with Kate on her communication and social skills. It is so fun to see her grow and develop in this area. Both of our older daughters attend the University of Kentucky here in Lexington. They often bring their friends out to the house for dinner and a visit. Their friends are very kind to Kate and have amazingly treated Kate as one of their own.

Kate senses their warmth and compassion, and feels very comfortable communicating with them. This allows Kate to be herself and, with that, you see her communication blossom.

When Kate is being herself, she cracks jokes and likes to share her stories. One day, our oldest daughter, Kala, asked, "Do you think Kate knows that she's actually pretty funny?" I said, "Oh yes she does, because the more you laugh, the more she pours it on."

Often it seems that everything you do turns out to be a therapy session. One of the ways we work on Kate's social and communication skills is by going out to dinner. When we eat out, we allow Kate and her sisters to order for themselves. Kate reads the menu and tells the waitress or waiter what she wants. If some assistance is needed we'll give it, but we do not take over the conversation and responsibility.

Kate is an adolescent girl who is growing and maturing like any typical girl. As we like to say, she is much more alike than different from a child without a disability. We have the same core goals and expectations for her as we do for our other kids. She experiences many of the same challenges that others face, both socially and intellectually. Like most, she's taking on her life with great zest and vigor, which would make any parent proud.

*Kala, Kelsey, and Kate, summer vacation, 2008*

*Kate, Kala and Kelsey having fun at a wedding party*

*Kala and Kate at 2009 Miss Kentucky pageant*

*Kelsey and Kate, 2010 summer vacation*

*Summer vacation at the beach 2008*

# THE OTHER TWO

As you now know by now, Kate is just one of our three daughters. I would be remiss if I didn't tell you a bit more about the other two. They have been the best big sisters that any little sister could ever desire.

Kate, like others her age, learns a lot from imitating the behavior of others. Kala and Kelsey helped shape and mold Kate into who she is today by being excellent examples and role models for her. They both have been a great inspiration for not only Kate but to Karen and me as well. As with all kids, they have their unique personalities and qualities that help shape, mold and define our family.

## *Kala*

Kala has always wanted to be her own person, blaze her own trail and try new things. Complying with the norm and having boundaries have not been her cup of tea. Kala is a soaring bird that doesn't want any limitations on what she can do or accomplish. If you focus this mentality and energy into positive ideas, goals and actions, the rewards can be endless.

Karen and I grew up in a small rural town and participated in the traditional extracurricular activities such as softball, baseball and basketball. We expected our kids to have the same general interests and lifestyles we had as kids. But that wouldn't be the case with Kala.

*Kerry Boudreaux*

Kala has always been on the move. From her adolescent years, her adventurous attitude has fueled her to participate in a vast array of activities from swimming, basketball, acting and Ultimate Frisbee. Her life goals and ambitions have been shaped and etched as well by this attitude. Her goal is to study abroad in Spain while obtaining her degree in international business and eventually have a career where she can travel the world.

Kala's attitude towards life has served her well. Both Karen and I observe her setting ambitious goals and aspirations, and cheer her on as she achieves them. We all know someone who makes the impossible seem so easy. Well, Kala is one of those people.

In October of 2009, Kala came to her mother and me and said she wanted to be in the Miss Teen Kentucky pageant. Her reason for doing it was simply, "Because I've always wanted to be in a pageant." I scoffed at the idea for two reasons. First, because all I could see was how much it was going to cost, and second, I was concerned that she wouldn't even come close to winning because she had never been in a beauty pageant. I felt it would result in her having a very bruised self-esteem that would need some serious mending.

It took a lot of coaxing and convincing by both her and her mother, but I agreed, with the only stipulation being that they wouldn't tell me how much it was going to cost; I just didn't need that heartache. So off they went, shopping and pageant practicing.

The pageant was held in December in Murray, Kentucky, on the Murray State University campus, just down the road from our hometown of Paducah, so our parents and family were able to come and watch. The pageant consisted of each girl modeling once in their evening gown and once in their swimsuit.

From there, the judges would pick the Top 15. These 15 would then make another appearance in their evening gowns, with the Top Five to be selected at this point. The final phase of the pageant consisted of the Top Five being interviewed, with the winner being chosen by the final top score from the judges.

We all got settled into our seats and the pageant began. There were a lot of pretty and elegant young girls in the pageant, but like most fathers, I thought mine was the most beautiful. With that I sat back, relaxed and looked forward to the show.

The girls had modeled their evening gowns and swimsuits, and the Top 15 were ready to be announced. I was completely stunned to hear Kala's name called. I was already tasting the crow that I was sure to be served for the next few weeks, since I was the "negative neigh Bob" from the very beginning. I was so very proud of her and could only imagine the joy and happiness that she must be feeling.

The second modeling performance was then conducted and the judges were ready to announce the final five. Not knowing anything about pageants I still had no expectations. Now, as I mentioned before, I was stunned when I heard Kala's name announced as part of the Top 15. When I say I almost had a heart attack when I heard her name announced as one of the Top Five would be an understatement. I just couldn't believe it. I laughed until I cried.

At this point they held the interview portion of the contest. Three girls went before Kala and did an exceptional job at answering their questions. I knew Kala would do extremely well with this as she is very comfortable with public speaking and being on stage. Sure enough, she knocked it out of the park. One of Karen's good friends and sorority sisters, who is a former Miss Kentucky, was sitting in front of us, turned and opined to us that Kala, "had just won the pageant with her fantastic answer." It was the first time that I really thought Kala was going to win.

There was one last girl. The final contestant in the interview portion was beautiful, elegant and very poised. In my opinion, she was the only one standing between Kala and Miss Teen Kentucky. She received her question and gave a very eloquent answer.

The five were brought back out for the most anticipated moments of any pageant, the process of announcing the winner. As they began announcing each runner-up, I kept expecting to hear Kala's name. As they worked their way through fourth, third and second, they did not call her name. My goodness, the final two included Kala. As the emcee began the announcement of the winner, my heart was beating faster than a jack rabbit running his trail. The envelope was opened and the emcee announced, "And the first runner-up is Kala Boudreaux!"

And if that wasn't enough, she was voted Miss Congeniality, to which her sister Kelsey leaned over to me and said, "Now that's a load of crap!" . . . True story.

What I had dismissed as a mere pretend experience to be Cinderella for a night turned out to be a life changing experience. This was only made possible by Kala's willingness to venture out of her comfort zone. An individual with a conforming mentality who doesn't want to try new things would have never accomplished what she did.

It's amazing how Kate has learned this particular trait from Kala. Kala loves her baby sister and they have a special bond. As their father, it's been really heartwarming to see Kala and Kate share their common traits and personalities as they grow and mature.

We recently took a short family vacation to Gatlinburg, Tennessee, where we did the typical family things of going to the theme and water parks. It was a wonderful trip for all of us, but especially for Kala and Kate. This was a tremendous opportunity for them to bond and grow their relationship and they both seized upon it. They rode rides and went down the water slides together. They went shopping, had lunch and ate dinner together.

From a parent's perspective, it was really nice to see Kala taking the time out of her busy schedule to be with her sister. Life is about these close relationships. Taking the time to nurture them should be important. Kate still talks about that weekend. It was a wonderful experience and one that we will cherish forever. She recently spent some time reflecting on her relationship with Kate and said I could share it with you.

*It was the summer of 1999 when my sister and I found out that we were going to be having a younger brother or sister. At the time I was eight and my sister, Kelsey, was seven. This sort of news to children of this age was filled with excitement like that of Christmas morning. We couldn't grasp the true excitement and responsibly of having an expectant mother and how much our family's life was about to change.*

*One of my fondest memories was how we shared the news with our grandparents that Mom was pregnant. One afternoon we were in the kitchen on one of our "girl afternoons" when we came across a recipe for fortune cookies. Each message could be personalized which were great for parties or for spilling important information if you catch my drift. We hurriedly cooked up our little surprise fortune cookies with our special message inside as Nana and Papaw were due to arrive for dinner that evening. I remember the table was set for six and thinking that in nine months it would be seven. The cookies were served at dinner and both Nana and Papaw chuckled at the unusual and creative masterpiece that my sister and I had created. As we each cracked our homemade fortune cookies we couldn't help but get a kick out of Nana and Papaw's reaction when they read the message. A new special angel was about to be a part of our family and we could not wait to see what this journey had in store for us.*

*Fast forward to March 24th 2000. Kelsey and I were patiently waiting in the hospital room as we watched the clock tick by, waiting for our little sister to arrive. We waited and waited until finally my grandparents decided to pack us both up and head home to wait and see what the morning would hold. We barely slept at all that night because we knew it couldn't be that much longer until she would enter into the world. Our little sister Kate was born at Centennial Hospital in Nashville, TN on March 25, 2000 around 6:30 a.m. We rushed to the hospital with our Nana and Papaw so excited that we could barely stand it. We arrived in the room where we found the nurse and our mom and dad casually talking but our little bundle of joy was nowhere to be found. The nurse sat us down and began to talk. She explained that Kate was born with Down syndrome, a fairly common genetic disorder. She described how it was just going to require a little more patience from my sister and I, but we were perfect for the job of being Kate's teachers. Being eight-and seven-years-old, we really couldn't wrap our minds around what this really meant. All we could think about was how we had a new baby sister that we couldn't wait to hold, feed, play games with and be role models for her.*

*And that was that; Kate had Down syndrome, in one ear and out the other from what I could remember. Kate was in the NICU unit for about a week so the doctors could more closely monitor her. Each day we would go visit her. Mom and Dad would let us hold and feed her, while they took our pictures with the instant Polaroid camera (nothing digital yet) so we could immediately see ourselves with her.*

*I'm sure I had a million questions of which I cannot recall as I write this, but what I do remember is not being scared, hesitant or embarrassed about having to go to the hospital just to see my new sister. I wasn't ashamed that my new sister wasn't "normal". The hospital staff made us feel welcome and Mom and Dad showed us from the outset what unconditional love looked and felt like. That was the foundation upon which we were going to raise and treat Kate; love her unconditionally and treat her no differently. Accept her differences and challenges as we accept everyone's differences and challenges.*

*From the beginning, I can only remember everyone talking about how we were going to give Kate as many opportunities as possible. We were going to treat and raise her no differently than we would any other child. Thirteen years later, we have not changed that attitude. Kate has been involved in countless number of activities such as dance, bowling, music and swimming. She rides her bike, enjoys going to the amusement and water parks, riding the roller coasters and going down the biggest and tallest slides. I couldn't be more proud Kate as I see her perform her cheerleading routine. I get a little teary eyed because I am so proud. I have never seen her get nervous before a choir performance or show, and I've never seen her back down from competing in a swim meet with everybody watching. There is a fearlessness that Kate embodies that I believe we can all learn from. She exemplifies courage and determination, and has a positive attitude in everything that she does. She doesn't let the fear of embarrassment or failure scare her. She competes with the "big kids" and takes pride in her work. Kate keeps a smile on her face and you can always find her with a hug or a high five, no matter who you are.*

*Kate has taught me so much despite the nine-year age difference. It is a warm, breezy summer evening as I write this from a balcony overlooking the beautiful city of Barcelona Spain. As I've reflected on my relationship with Kate these past few days, I recall some of the obstacles that I've had to overcome while living here. The things that make me uncomfortable, the things that cause me frustration and stress, and put me in a bad mood such as the language barrier or not fully understanding the proper thing to do because I fully don't understand the message, are things that Kate has to encounter on a daily basis. These are things that Kate will have to overcome for the rest of her life. This has given me a better appreciation for Kate's positive attitude and*

**gives me a glimpse of what life might be like looking through her prism.**

## *Kelsey*

From the day Kate was born, Kelsey has had a special bond with her baby sister. She found it interesting how the therapists worked with Kate, particularly how they took special care with her. It was interesting to see how Kelsey, at such a young age, recognized the compassion they had for Kate in their work. As I mentioned earlier, it was these early impressions that led Kelsey to her career choice.

Kelsey is extremely grounded and centered. From her early childhood, we witnessed a very thoughtful child who had a very caring heart, whether it was for her friends or her sisters. She enjoyed her quiet time and seemed to use it to reflect. In grade school, we were blessed with reflective thoughts which she put in writing, whether through personal letters to us, birthday messages or reflective narratives.

Kelsey has always been a "late bloomer." She didn't get her first tooth until she was 17 months old and her head had very little hair for the longest time, which garnered her nickname, "Peach Fuzz." She was the smallest in her class until her freshman year of high school. That's when the growth spurt hit.

Through grade school, she enjoyed playing guitar. She also played on the grade-school basketball team and was a very accomplished swimmer. When she was finishing the eighth grade, she decided she wanted to try cheerleading. I wasn't much for it as I thought it was going to be just a passing thing, but to my surprise, she loved it and was on the cheerleading squad all during high school.

Along with her extracurricular activities, Kelsey is an excellent student. Carrying a 3.8 GPA in high school is not easy, and to continue it through four semesters of college as a kinesiology major, earning her Dean's List honors, is even more impressive.

Kelsey always keeps a special place in her heart for those who may not be as fortunate, whether financially, physically, emotionally or intellectually. If she sees that someone needs help or a kind word, or just needs to be included, she's there. I see these traits coming from her experience of having a sibling with a disability. These insights and perspectives may not have been gained without this special relationship.

During our recent work on the Brighter Tomorrows project, Kelsey offered the follow reflection on her relationship with Kate.

*I was six years old when my little sister Kate was born. When my parents told me she had Down syndrome, I didn't get scared or think any different of her. She was still a cute little bundle of joy and all I cared about was the fact that I was a brand new big sister!*

*After a few months, I realized that Kate was going to need a little extra help with some things that I never needed help with when I was a baby. Kate started with her therapy around eight weeks old; she had speech therapy, occupational therapy and physical therapy. The therapy was supposed to be for Kate, but my older sister Kala and I always attended the therapy sessions because they were so much fun! My personal favorite was when Kate had physical therapy. It amazed me that the physical therapist could create Kate's therapy around games that were fun for all three of us sisters. It amazed me so much that it is actually my career choice now. Experiencing Kate's therapy with her made me want to be able to give that same joy to another little boy or girl with Down syndrome as well as their siblings and families.*

*Today, Kate might possibly be the funniest, sassiest and most normal 12-year-old little sister I have ever met in my life. She is in the regular fifth-grade class at her school and does everything that every other kid does. She is always singing, dancing, playing the piano, riding her bike, jumping on the trampoline or talking about how excited she is for middle school next year. She has speech therapy on Mondays, piano lessons on Wednesdays and dance (hip hop, jazz, ballet and tap) on Thursdays—and she loves every minute of it.*

*We have had our struggles as a family, but what family hasn't? No family is perfect, but we are always there for each other and we always love each other no matter what. Having a little sister with Down syndrome is no different than having a little sister with no disability. She still steals my clothes (and they actually fit her), she gets under my skin, she goes in my room when I don't want her to, and she NEVER lets me have the front seat in the car. Regardless, I love Kate to death and I would never, ever want a different little sister.*

Karen and I have been truly gifted with three wonderful daughters. They have an exceptional bond that never would have been formed had it not been for Kate and Down syndrome. They have experiences that are unique and will serve them well in their life.

# GRANDPARENTS

One goal for most of us is retiring and "enjoying the grandkids," as they say. I'm not a grandparent yet, but with two daughters past their teens I suppose I'm not that far off. After watching our parents work their grandparent magic over the years, I've come to realize that, like most things in life, being a good grandparent requires lots of time and special care.

Many things change, but many things remain the same. No matter how old we get, we always want the best for our kids. We want them to be happy and free of worry and problems. We'll always see ourselves as their protector, looking to keep them from harm's way and looking to shelter them from the burdens of life. We are always willing to take away any pain or sorrow that may come their way and are always willing to shoulder it ourselves. No matter how old they are, we'll do these things.

When Kate was born, one of the challenges I had was sharing with our parents that their new grandchild had Down syndrome. Though I was comfortable with the diagnosis and immediately accepted our new child unconditionally, I wasn't sure how they would react to the news. It wasn't because I didn't think they would love Kate any less, rather it was because there was so much anticipation of having a new grandchild that I didn't want the fact that Kate had Down syndrome to be "bad" news in an otherwise joyous occasion.

You see, everyone says that they don't care if it's a boy or girl; they just want a healthy baby. I wanted our parents to think that Kate was a healthy baby, but everyone's perception is that a baby with Down syndrome is not healthy, which is not at all true. I thought if they felt Kate was not a healthy baby, they would worry for us and for her. They would carry the burden, and the happiness that one feels over a newborn child would be diminished. I didn't want them to feel they had to shoulder any portion of the perceived "burden" or "problem." I didn't think they deserved that responsibility.

I remember being especially concerned about how I was going to share the news with my parents. You see, my sister—who lived in Oklahoma, some 12 hours away from us in Nashville—was expecting her first child at the same time. In fact, Kate and my niece, Hanna, just happened to be born on the same day.

We agreed that my parents should be in Oklahoma for Hanna's birth, then travel to Nashville to visit with us. My dilemma; we have the diagnosis, Kate's in NICU for a week before we can bring her home, and my parents are in Oklahoma celebrating the joy of their only daughter giving birth to her first child. How and when was I going to tell them? My thought was I didn't want to "rain on their parade."

My fear and concern were rooted in my ignorance, as I didn't have any experience in dealing with this type of situation. What I did have was a wife with infinite wisdom. I'm sure it was from her motherly instincts, but she was confident and secure in knowing not only how she would share the news, but that our parents would be safe and their new granddaughter would receive the same love and attention that their other grandchildren received.

It was her firm belief that our parents, and others, would react however we presented it. If we presented Down syndrome in a negative way, they would receive it in a negative way. If we presented Down syndrome as an opportunity for us all to grow and learn, then they would accept it that way.

Karen was correct in her assessment. Karen and I never once presented Down syndrome as "bad" news. We never once presented Kate as a diagnosis. Once again, Kate is a person. Kate is a child, a miracle, just like everyone else. She just happens to have Down syndrome, just like a person just happens to have blue eyes or brown hair.

Our parents and family accepted Kate as a child, not as a diagnosis. She has had such tremendous love and support from her grandparents and extended family. No one has ever seen Down syndrome as "bad" news. They have embraced Kate as another family member, and she has embraced them.

Our kids and their grandparents enjoy many special moments together. We've always lived several hours away, so, like most, we've had to make family a real priority to allow our kids to develop relationships with their grandparents. We've been very fortunate to have the opportunity to share most birthdays, holidays and other special occasions with our families.

Nothing means more to grandparents and their grandkids than time spent together doing simple things like eating ice cream or baking a cake, cookies or a pie. Over the years, the kids have spent hours playing board and card games with their grandparents. These are cherished times and have been the catalyst for the strong, loving bond between them.

Kate has enjoyed wonderful relationships with her grandparents. Until the passing of her grandfathers (my father in June of 2008 from cancer and Karen's father in October 2012 from ALS), Kate and her "Pawpaw Boudreaux" and "Papaw AJ" were all close buddies. Kate was known to them as their little sunshine as she always brightened their day. You see, when both were going through their illnesses, Kate would go visit and greet them with a big hearty smile and a, "Hello there sunshine!" She always had a way of brightening their day with her cheery disposition, coupled with a sweet kiss on the cheek and a big hug.

Kate has meant so much to her grandmothers as well. They each recently sent me a note regarding their relationship with Kate and I wanted to share them with you.

*Reflection from "Mimi" Boudreaux (my mother)*

*For those that have not had the opportunity to meet Kate, you are missing out on a gift of Love and Hope! She loves unconditionally and her smile is like a ray of sunshine. Her eyes twinkle like the stars when she meets you. Kate loves to perform and can easily learn her part. She does not expect you to be perfect but does expect herself to be perfect. Maybe we all need an extra chromosome. I am looking forward and anxious to be here for her teen years.*

*Mimi*

*Reflection from "Nana" Roof (Karen's mother)*

*Our Special Angel*

*On March 25, 2000, a special angel entered our world. She was born to our daughter and son-in-law. Her name is Katheryn (Kate). Soon after she was born, her parents were informed that she had been diagnosed with Down syndrome. When they told us, my husband and I immediately thought back to my family of nine siblings and his family of ten (10). Neither of us grew up knowing a child with special needs.*

*We know that having a baby is a miracle and a gift from God. Healthy babies are born every day and we don't think much about it except that another miracle has happened. Our faith has always made us realize that God knows best and that he chooses special parents to care for any special needs child. He chooses parents who both are patient, kind, loving and giving, who will love the child with all their hearts and will give the child all the love and care that it needs. In all of my years of living we do know that many parents don't fit that description.*

*Since we are Kate's grandparents, we felt that God chose us, too, to love her and to help care for her the very best we can. Even though we had quite a scare when she was taken to the intensive care unit the same day she was born, she turned out to be a very healthy little girl.*

*Kate is a very special little angel who brings so much joy to us. With the help of therapists who are so well-trained she has learned so much more than we could ever imagine that she could learn by this age. Whenever we talk to Karen on the phone and Kate is close by, she always wants to talk. Sometimes she even takes the phone to her mother and says to her, "Nana-Papaw", so that her mom will call us to talk. That truly makes our day special.*

*Even though we don't live in the same town, Kate has never forgotten us from one trip to the next. Believe me, she will succeed in life. She is so special and precious that she makes friends with everyone she meets. Our granddaughter is so precious to us that we could never imagine her being any different than she is and we would not want her to be any different. She is our very special gift from God and we are so thankful for her.*

*Kate is now 13 years old. She attends school and has learned so much from the wonderful teachers and aides who have worked with her. It is so amazing, too, that she has learned several outside activities. She dances beautifully and does quite well in her recitals. She swims and almost caused her parents to have a heart attack when she jumped into the pool for the first time at the deep end and came up swimming like a little fish.*

*She loves singing and is a member of the chorus group in school. She joined Special Olympics cheerleading. I went to their national competition in Atlanta. I could have never believed how good they were had I not watched them for myself. It was such a beautiful experience and they all worked very hard.*

*Last summer, Kate helped me take care of her grandfather, who had to be put in the nursing home. Kate knew that that "Papaw" was very sick but she never missed a chance to visit him in the hospital. She would make sure his cup was always full of water and she wanted to help feed him. Anytime Kate walked into the room he would always smile at her, no matter how bad he felt. It meant so much to him to see her each time. She was like a dose of medicine for him.*

*Her "Papaw" died in October of 2012 and she misses him so much. Each time I see her she is asking me if I am OK and she says she misses her "Papaw". She tells us that "Papaw" went to help Jesus and He will help him watch over us.*

From Day One, we've seen Down syndrome for what it is; a true blessing in our life. Many people would say we are the best example of, "when God gives you lemons, make lemonade." This could not be further from the truth. What God has given us is an endless supply of the finest wine money can buy, and we've decided to share it with everyone we meet.

# SPIRITUAL LIFE

Karen and I were both reared in Catholic homes. We were enrolled in Catholic schools and attended Mass weekly, many times more than once a week as we had daily Mass before school. For each of our families, Sunday Mass attendance was part of vacations if the vacation covered the Sabbath. That once bugged me a bit and I challenged my mother with it. Her reply was a simple, "Do you want God to take a vacation from helping you?" She had an excellent point, as she usually did, and it has stuck in my mind for over 40 years.

Our spiritual foundation has certainly helped carry us through the many challenges over the years. It's also helped us realize and honor the many wonderful blessings which we have been given. We don't spend a lot of time memorizing Bible verses and reciting them to stake out a position or case, but we do spend a lot of time reading the Bible for guidance, understanding and perspective. We spend a lot of time in quiet spiritual reflection, and regularly pray for our family and friends through daily heart prayers. We pray for our deceased fathers daily, asking them for guidance and a watchful eye.

All of our kids received their sacraments and each practices their faith. Kate was baptized as an infant and received first communion when she was in the third grade. She participates in weekly Mass and assists with the offertory, as our parish has a tradition of allowing the children to take up the collection. This has been an excellent way for Kate to share her talents with the church.

The church staff does a wonderful job of working with her. As Kate participates by passing the collection basket down each row, you can see the warm and loving smiles from the congregation. If I see it and feel it, I know Kate can, too.

We do have grace before meals and if our bedtime routine doesn't turn into a five-alarm fire drill, bedtime prayers are said each evening. Our bedtime prayers are a combination of a very short formal prayer followed by each person saying something that they are sorry for, then something for which they are thankful, then closing with those people for whom we want to especially pray. As I mentioned before, there are many times adult words cross our lips, and these are overheard by the little ears.

As you know, kids are like parrots, and Kate is no exception. Needless to say, these "garbage words" get repeated. Well, during bedtime prayers Kate often says that she is sorry for the "garbage words" she has said over the course of the day.

One evening she said she was sorry for saying "garbage words" that day. She then decided to recite the very words she was sorry for saying, catching us completely off-guard! We started laughing, and the more we laughed the more she said them!

Karen and I help our kids build a strong spiritual relationship with God. Until recently, I often wondered if Kate would ever have a true spiritual relationship with God and understand the whole concept of religion. I knew we would ensure that she attended church on a regular basis, but would she have that spiritual relationship?

My concerns were founded on the fact she learns and comprehends best if what she is learning is tangible. Intangible concepts—things that she can't see, smell or taste—are much more difficult, if not impossible, for her to learn and understand. A spiritual relationship with God is certainly an intangible concept, or so I thought.

This was especially troubling for me because I firmly believe one needs to have a strong spiritual relationship with God. I think it's the core to your moral compass. Without it, life is meaningless. I didn't want Kate to miss having that relationship.

Recently, we started attending Mass at the Newman Center on the University of Kentucky campus. Kate's friend Megan, who I introduced you to earlier, and her family, call it their home parish and attend Mass each Sunday. We've had the privilege of getting to know them over the years, but we'd never attended Mass on a regular basis with them.

It has been quite a life-changing experience for me. Megan participates in the Mass as an altar server and Eucharistic minister, and helps take up the collection. She takes her duties very seriously and is most reverent in her prayers.

The main thing I have noticed is that Megan is very spiritual. She takes quiet time for reflection during Mass and you can certainly tell that she is focused on developing her relationship with God. It was here that I found my answer. It was here that my eyes were opened. It was here that Megan taught me to see things totally differently with Kate.

When you receive communion, you are receiving the body of Christ. If you happen to receive communion from Megan when she's the Eucharistic minister of the Body, you realize that you are receiving the Bread of Life through her. As you stand before her, you have the quick moment to peer into her eyes and you quickly realize that God is present in her heart and soul. You realize that the Body and Spirit are being presented to you through her. You realize that God must be present in her and with her. This, I'm sure, led me to the answer that yes, Kate can and will have a relationship with God.

Now when I look around, I realize that Kate is in constant relationship with God. She is the vessel that God works through each and every day. Kate sees "Godness" in everyone. She always has a smile and hug for everyone she meets. Her spiritual life is living and sharing God with others. She's living His word, each and every day, and I didn't see it. It was right there before me. I should have known God wouldn't allow one of his children to miss having a relationship with Him.

# MAKE SURE YOU
# FOLLOW THE SIGNS

The pathway through life is full of wonder and splendor, and filled with happiness and joy. It can, however, be difficult to navigate if you lose your direction. On life's path, we are given many signs to follow. Some are quite obvious, while others are not.

So what do I mean by following the signs? Well, two things. First, we've all been faced with decisions to make—some big, some small—and we just don't know what to do. No matter how much we analyze it, we just can't always determine which decision is best.

When Karen and I find ourselves in this situation, we often look for signs—spiritual signs, if you will. We essentially offer up the decision to a "Higher" being, asking Him to provide us with His answer and guidance.

Second, some things just randomly happen in our lives that just don't make much sense. Again, these events could be big or small. If you're not looking for them, they just pass you by. My experience tells me to be vigilant for these signs. Look, pray and ask for them.

When Kala and Kelsey were in middle school, a local parish church, St. Elizabeth Ann Seton, was opening a new school and we were considering moving them there. We were pleased with where the kids were going to school and there wasn't real need for a change.

The new Seton school was going to be a state-of-the-art facility. The new principal had a wonderful reputation, and the commute was 10 minutes closer. It was the end of July and we really needed to make a decision as the new school was to open in a month and the classes were filling up fast.

As with most decisions regarding our children—especially when their education and faith development are concerned—we found this to be an extremely difficult choice. Our summer vacation was upon us, so we decided to take some time to relax and give us a chance to discuss it.

As we always do on vacation, we attended Sunday Mass at a local church. After communion, I decided to stand at the back of the church instead of going back to the pew. After some quiet reflection and the closing prayer, I began observing the unique surroundings in the narthex. There was a small statue, in a shadow box, of a lady reading to some young girls. The caption on the box explained that the statue was St. Elizabeth Ann Seton. I never knew who St. Elizabeth Ann Seton was and I had never seen a statue of her.

After Mass I immediately went and got Karen and brought her over to show her what I had found. A month later our kids were attending St. Elizabeth Ann Seton School and nine months later, Kala was a member of the first graduating class.

To explain how signs are given to us on a more random and obscure basis, I offer this example. I have a ceramic statue of Jesus in my office. As I was cleaning my credenza one day, I knocked the statue over onto the hardwood floor.

For all practical purposes, the entire statue should have shattered because it landed on a solid oak floor, but only the hands broke off. Karen quickly sought out the glue and was ready to mend it back together.

However, I wasn't in such a hurry to make the repairs. You see, I found it odd that this delicate, ceramic statue had taken a tumble but only the hands were broken. I wanted some time to reflect on what had happened, not so much from a physics perspective but from a meaningful and spiritual perspective. Was there a sign that I should be receiving here? Was this telling me something?

Karen agreed to leave my "handless" Jesus alone, allowing it to be a focal point and a reminder for me to seek out the daily signs.

Each day since that event, I've entered my office to see the handless Jesus. After careful reflection over several months, I came to this conclusion. You see, God gave us His word through the prophets and His Son. These words are what form the Bible. They are forever scribed for all to see and read, to the end of time.

To *teach* us and to do His work here on earth, God gave us His only Son. Jesus, being in the likeness of man, was mortal. He had 33 years to physically be with us to carry out God's work. Jesus did all he could here on earth to show us how to carry out God's work, but being in the likeness of man, He could not be here forever. With that, God needs each of us to continue to carry out His works. He needs us to be His hands. Yes, His words need to be spread, but without our hands fulfilling His words, they are just words.

You see, if I wasn't looking for signs, I would have missed this sign and the and many others. that have been given to help guide me. Many of these signs are given to us and we just can't explain or understand them. I suggest seeking counsel and guidance, whether a close friend, family member or a professional; they can give you a different perspective, a different understanding. They can shine a different light or paint the picture in way that you can better understand.

Soon after my father passed away in 2008, I had a very vivid dream in which he appeared to me. To this day it seemed so real that I felt he was in my midst. In this dream, he was so excited and happy. He was telling me that heaven was a real place and it was beautiful.

To prove it to me, he held out his hands and upon his palms were emblazoned crosses.

I often think about that dream. I've never had a dream so real, so vivid. The colors are etched in my mind. I keep thinking that there is some meaning, some sign from that dream. Was it just to ensure me that heaven is real? Was it a sign that I am on the right path and to continue on my journey with the same convictions, hopes and dreams? Was it to say that I need to help carry the crosses and burdens of my family and my fellow brothers and sisters?

For several days I stayed vigilant to try and learn from that dream. I finally shared it with Karen and she offered some great insight. She said my father is looking out for me and that I should put any problems into God's hands. Any crosses that I am asked to bear, He will help me carry them. No cross is too heavy and no cross is too burdensome.

God has my dad in heaven now as my guardian angel. When any cross I am being asked to carry just seems too heavy, I can call on him and lay it in his hands and he will help.

I look back over all the years and wonder if certain events, chance meetings or relationships were given to me as a way of preparing my heart and soul for Kate. Were they signs of what my life would hold? Was meeting Tommy at such an early age and developing our friendship a sign of what lay ahead for me? I look back on it and say, yes, most certainly.

Was meeting a college student who was blind but studied, worked and lived a completely independent life a way to educate me on the possibilities of people with disabilities and to shape my attitude towards them? The answer again is yes—why else would I still have him in my memory 30 years later?

Nobody knows what the future holds, but being able to reflect back and observe the past, then see how it has molded the present and how it can shape the future, is a wonderful feeling. It gives you hope for the future and solitude for the past.

Karen and I have been chosen by God to love and nurture three of His very special gifts, our three children. At times, it's not easy. At times, we wonder what is best, what is good. As with everyone, we need special guidance along our path. I know this guidance will be given to us; it always has been and it always will be. We need to look for the signs; they will be there, they have been and always will be there. We must vigilant, we must be aware. We look for them and we pray for them. They are there, each and every day.

# THEY KNOW WHO THEY ARE

Growing up with Tommy, I often wondered how he perceived things and how he felt about them. I often wondered if he had the typical emotions of sadness, happiness, anger, etc. I often wondered if he knew there was a difference in how he talked or how he learned compared to how a typical person performs these tasks. Did he *know* he had Down syndrome?

Shortly after Kate was born I got my answer to all of the above questions. Karen and I had the opportunity to attend a Down syndrome conference in Chicago. From all the wonderful seminars and break-out sessions, I got the most out of the talent show which was held one evening.

There were a couple of reasons I enjoyed the event so much. First, to see kids perform dance routines of tap, jazz and ballet, play the piano—not just a simple musical piece, but Beethoven, Bach and Chopin—was absolutely astonishing to me. I never knew people with Down syndrome had the ability, both physically and intellectually, to accomplish what they were doing. It was a profound moment that totally changed my paradigm.

The second reason it was such an enlightening evening for me was one particular act. A young man, probably in his late teens, had written a song and performed it in the musical sway of the day, rap. But he didn't just sing it—he performed it.

This young man laid out his heart in this performance, and in so doing he answered all my questions. He sang of his hopes and dreams, as well as the challenges that he faced each and every day. He spoke and sang about having Down syndrome.

One verse I can never get out of my head is about him not having a lot of friends because of Down syndrome. All he wanted was to be included with his groups of friends. He sang about wanting to be included in parties and games, and he asked people not to look at him differently or treat him differently because he has Down syndrome.

This wasn't just an isolated incident. I started to experience others. Several months later we were back in Paducah for a family visit. Kate was about a year old and we were attending church one Sunday morning.

A high school classmate of mine has a brother, Tim, with Down syndrome, and he was in his late 30's at this particular time. We met Tim and his mother after church to catch up on things and chat, as is typical, after Sunday service. Tim's mother, Kaye, wanted to hold Kate while Tim observed. Tim was able to hold Kate as well, which he loved. The visit finished up with hugs and kisses and normal good-byes.

A few weeks later, we were back in Paducah and ran into Tim's mother. We exchanged pleasantries and she told us of a conversation she'd had with Tim after our visit at church a few weeks earlier. She said they were driving home and talking about Kate. Tim spoke about how sweet Kate was, and then told his mother, "You know, Kate looks like me, doesn't she, Mom?"

Kaye told us that that Tim knows he has Down syndrome and he knows when someone else does, too. She said he is very sensitive to it and is very aware. When I met Tim the next time, we gave each other our customary handshakes and hugs, and exchanged pleasantries. He asked about Kate, and to this day always does.

As Kate has grown and matured, all of my other questions have been answered as well. She has experienced her own share of ups and downs, just like any child does. She gets bored, loves to have friends and feels inferior when she's left out of a group or conversation. She gets mad when she doesn't get her way or loses a game, and is happy and excited when she accomplishes her goals. She's experienced the loss of a loved one and feels the sadness just like we do. She experiences all of these emotions, no differently than anyone else.

Once again, from brief moments and chance meetings, and from raising my own child with Down syndrome, I have learned so much more than I ever learned from reading a book, taking a class or attending a seminar. I look back on my initial curiosities and unanswered questions, and think, how silly of me to think that just because of Kate's disability she wouldn't have the same type of emotions as a typical child.

We often forget that Kate and others with Down syndrome are people just like you and me. They are not a diagnosis, and we should not treat them that way. I learned some valuable lessons from the rap singer, as well as from Tim and Kate and Kate herself—lessons that I use myself. I use these lessons every day in raising Kate and in communicating and interacting with people who have a disability.

# ELEVEN UNDENIABLE TRUTHS OF REARING A CHILD WITH SPECIAL NEEDS

1. Patience. This virtue is needed above all others.
2. People with special needs will run the same race, just at a different pace.
3. People with special needs are human beings with a diagnosis, not a diagnosis that happens to be a human being.
4. We are not alone. We are not the first, nor the last, to have a child with special needs. Seek counsel and guidance. Use it and pass it along.
5. Not everyone is going to be a rocket scientist. Understand their abilities and maximize them. Encourage and expect greatness within their capabilities, just like you do your other kids.
6. Spend equal time, if not more, in developing social skills as you do in developing intellectual skills. Friends and family are just as important as reading, writing and arithmetic.
7. Don't feel sorry, either for ourselves or them. We've been given special gifts and blessings in disguise. We must recognize them and help them grow and flourish.
8. A strong family unit is needed more than ever. Pray, play and work together.
9. We all want the best for our kids. Advocate for them. Give them another voice, so they can advocate for themselves one day.
10. A child with special needs will influence more lives by the time they're a teenager than most people will in a lifetime.
11. Don't judge a person's intellectual capability by their ability to communication

# THE HITS KEEP ON COMING

As I have mentioned throughout this writing, there are so many life lessons and special moments that my entire family has experienced because of Kate. Without her, as she is, these experiences would never have happened. My family would not be what it is today without Kate. My entire family would view things completely different, and I would submit that it would be for the worse, not the better.

I am not saying they would be viewing things badly, but I am saying they would not be viewing things as they do now. They would not have the same perspective on life.

By now, you've seen many great things happen because of Kate. There are many wonderful stories to be told at family gatherings. Without Kate, these stories would not be possible.

Special family moments are preserved in these stories. I share this for the same reason as mentioned before; I want you to see someone's disability not as a diagnosis, but as a trait that defines them. Kate has made our family special; she has made it unique. Down syndrome helps define her and it helps define our family and our community.

There are some great family stories involving Kate. I would love to share all of them with you, but for the sake of time, I will share only two. I still remember them as if they happened yesterday.

## *Kate throws out the first pitch*

When Kate was around two she was asked to throw out the first pitch for our minor league baseball team here in Lexington. Ronald McDonald, the McDonald's restaurant mascot, was there to assist with the event. Now, Ronald McDonald, when "on stage," is always Ronald McDonald; he does not come out of character. He is held to the same rule much like a Disney character—while they are visible in public, they must remain in character, regardless of what happens.

While we were waiting for the festivities to begin, Ronald was playing with Kate down on the field. It was very close to game time and they were getting ready to sing the national anthem. About four thousand people were in their seats when, all of a sudden Kate, who was standing next to Ronald McDonald, raises her dress because her diaper had slipped off.

Right there, in front of Ronald and all of those people, Kate is standing buck naked, and wouldn't put her dress down. I look up and Ronald McDonald has come completely out of character and is laughing while at the same time trying to cover his eyes. He doesn't know what to do.

I'm in the stands and Karen's screaming at me to go get Kate, but there are people all around and I couldn't get to her. People are innocently laughing and we as parents are in a complete panic. We finally get to Kate, Ronald McDonald does his best to regain his composure and character, and Kate completes her mission by throwing out the first pitch. The picture which they took of her (with diaper on and dress pulled down) still hangs on her bedroom wall.

## *Just go with it*

In Lexington, there's a small community newspaper that publishes local neighborhood stories and events. One of their annual features, called, "Notable Neighbors," recognizes people in the area for their outstanding community service and volunteer work. One year Karen was nominated and eventually selected based on her volunteer work with DSACK.

The publication sent a reporter to conduct the interview, and then sent a photographer to the house for some pictures. Karen selected the outfits to wear and the locations for the photos. We have a nice lake in our neighborhood and that's where Karen wanted to have the pictures taken.

When the photographer arrived, however, he had different plans. He looked around the house and the yard, and decided that it would be a great idea for Karen and the girls to lie down on the deck with their heads together while he got a shot of them from above. Karen hated the idea and pleaded to go to the lake for the shoot. Karen and the photographer compromised and did both shoots—one on the deck and one at the lake.

The following month, the special issue hit the newsstands all across town. The picture of Karen and the girls was beautiful, but it was not the one Karen had requested. In fact, the deck photo appeared on the front page of the newspaper! For the next month, everywhere we went sat this newspaper, for everyone to see . . . quite humorous, I thought.

Several months later, the National Down Syndrome Society was having its national Buddy Walk fundraiser in New York City. The organization sent out a request for photos that could be displayed on the jumbo TV at Times Square during their walk.

One of the DSACK board members loved our picture so much they sent it to NDSS, and the group selected it as part of its display. This time it was on display for millions of people to see—even more humorous, I thought.

Karen has finally decided she likes that picture. One of our neighbors even cut it out of the newspaper, laminated it and sent it to us with a note about how much he enjoyed the photo.

*Southsider magazine, "Most Notable Neighbors" edition 2007,*
***Smiley Pete Publishing.***
***Photo by Mick Jeffries***

# COURAGEOUS AND BRAVE

For me, the true meanings of the words, "courageous" and "brave" have always been reserved for the men and women who have served our country. They signed up for a job that asks them to **FIGHT,** which will put them to be put in harm's way to protect you and me, so that we may live free and have our individual liberty.

These words are thrown around a bit too easily, in my opinion. Using these words too frequently devalues their true meaning. These words should be preserved to describe truly courageous acts and those that have shown to be truly brave.

I never really heard these words describe Kate or any other person with a disability until I was talking with Caroline, my elementary and high school classmate, whose daughter, Callie, has Down syndrome. They live in Lexington and Callie is couple years older than Kate, so we often get together and visit, whether for lunch or a play date for the kids. The conversation tends to revolve around our kids and what they are experiencing. During one recent visit, Caroline was sharing with us the trials and tribulations of middle school and Callie's transition to adolescence.

Caroline shared with us a number of different things that were going on in Callie's life. Callie was beginning to notice that she wasn't as smart, or as fast or as strong as the other kids. She had come to perceive that she was different. Caroline described how Callie was coping with these perceptions, and that it was a bit of a struggle for her, to say the least.

Callie expressed her feelings with Caroline on a regular basis, talking of her differences and how hard it was to understand why she wasn't quite the same as the other students. Caroline said one of the ways that she was coping was by saying she didn't want to play with any of those kids that have a "Down syndrome" face. This was her way of thinking that she didn't have Down syndrome and she wasn't different than the other kids.

Now, where is the courage and bravery in that, you may ask? Just like Kate, Callie gets up every day with a great attitude and an incredible zest to take on the day. She grabs her breakfast and dashes off to her destination, clicking her heels and wearing a smile that would brighten anyone's day. Then, at the end of the day, with what seems like the same energy and vigor, she shares with you her joy and wonderful experiences which she encountered throughout the day.

I think we can all remember the difficulties of those adolescent years. Our voices and bodies were changing, school work was getting harder and the social scene was about as awkward as it could, and would ever get for us.

For any typical adolescent, these were difficult times. I now ask you to consider how you would have dealt with your adolescent years, had you been given the following, "add-ons:"

- You had an intellectually developmental delay and had to go to special resource classes each day of school. On top of your homework, you had speech, physical and occupational therapies.
- You had difficulty speaking, thus causing communication barriers with your peers, teachers, etc.
- You looked different. You weren't as "pretty" as your peer (in your peers' eyes)
- You were physically the slowest, weakest and least coordinated, often being the last person picked to be on the team. And when you did compete, you always finished last.

I would submit that you probably would have dealt with it much like I would have dealt with it, which is to say not very well at all. I think I would have been extremely depressed and lonely.

But that's not how Callie, Kate and other kids with disabilities deal with it. It is incredible to see their strength and boldness. It is incredible how they go through life with this "alligator skin" mentality. It seems nothing penetrates their positive attitude and outlook on life. They grab each day by the horns and live it as if it were their last.

Any challenge or obstacle thrown their way is attacked with a great spirit and attitude. I never would have thought that bravery and courageousness could be used to describe someone who has a disability, but after seeing the experiences of a child with special needs on a day-to-day basis, I certainly consider them to be extremely courageous and brave.

I think Caroline said it best. She told me Callie was having one of her moments where she was not feeling up to the challenges. As part of her consolation, she told Callie how proud she was of her and that she was such a brave and courageous girl. Callie liked that, regained her positive outlook and spirit, and went on about her day. Caroline, like we've done many times, went to the other room and cried. If her tears were similar to the ones I've shed in those situations, they were tears of sorrow. Sorrow for the pain and loneliness that our children must be enduring, coupled with the desire that we could take on that pain for them so that they could live a "normal" life. I only wish we had the courage and bravery that our kids display on a daily basis.

# HEARTS FILLED WITH PRIDE

Kate and I enjoy going out on a father-daughter date to the "dinner and a movie" theater. This is where you eat dinner while watching a movie. It's a really cool concept and Kate knows it's a special treat.

On one of our recent dates, we met one of Kate's friends, Jeremy, who works at the theatre. Jeremy is 24 years old and has Down syndrome. Kate was on Jeremy's Special Olympics softball team a few years ago, but we really didn't know him on a personal basis. He was working at the ticket counter, helping with tasks such as handing out menus, passing out and taking up tickets, and doing general customer service. Kate and I were about 45 minutes early for the movie, so we sat at the snack bar and ordered an appetizer of chips and dip, and something to drink. The place was not too busy, so I found this time to be a great opportunity to just with Jeremy and we got each other a bit better.

Jeremy stands about five feet, two inches tall and weighs 168 pounds (he told me so). He wears wire-rimmed glasses which go very well with his closely cropped haircut. Jeremy was wearing his nicely pressed slacks and golf shirt with the movie theatre's logo on the right breast. His shirt was neatly tucked in under a leather belt. His ensemble was completed by a nice pair of finely polished black shoes. He could have passed any Marine Corps inspection.

Something struck me as I watched Jeremy work. It was quite amazing to see him go from customer to customer and from task to task, making sure everything was in place and everyone was satisfied. He greeted people with a smile and his body language exuded great self-confidence. His gait was solid and steady with his shoulders pulled back and his head and eyes combing the room for an opportunity to serve.

I could not find the words to accurately describe what I saw as I watched Jeremy at work. I wanted to use the word, "pride," but that one didn't seem to fit. I needed something more to describe what I saw in Jeremy. I searched the thesaurus and found such words as, "arrogant," "conceited" and even, "highfaluting," but I knew this wasn't what I was seeing.

I wanted something that more accurately described Jeremy and what his work displayed, so I looked for other words. I didn't have to look very far. In the following sections the words, "humility," "servility" and "modesty" were headlined. Under these sections, I found such words as, "meek," "apple-polisher" and "unostentatious."

I was getting close, but I still didn't have a word that completely and wholly described Jeremy. I finally realized that I wasn't going to find "one" word that best described him. Jeremy was too good for just one word.

Jeremy, I decided, was a full dose of pride, with a slight sprinkle of meekness, a small dose of apple-polisher and a slight cut of unostentatious. He was not arrogant, but extremely confident. He was not conceited, but very selfless. He was very caring and made sure he was doing the very best job that anyone could possible do. He was taking great pride in his work and he was very proud of himself for accomplishing his goal of doing a good job.

After that chance encounter, my eyes have been opened a bit further as I now see how others with special needs take great pride in their work and what they do. Kate recently joined the Special Olympics cheerleading team and they too exude a tremendous amount of pride in their performances. They understand winning and losing. They understand the concept of teamwork. They understand the fact that they have to put in a lot of time and effort if they want to perform at a high level.

When I see teammates displaying leadership traits that you pine for in your own workforce or on your typical sports team, that tells me they understand core principle concepts such as pride, commitment, dedication and teamwork.

I find it very humbling to see how committed these folks are to achieving greatness. They are not seeking it, but they are achieving it. I suppose that's how greatness is attained; doing the small things each and every day to the best of your ability and before you know it, you've accomplished something that is unique, something that is considered to be of greatness.

These are the fundamentals to success in life. I see them thriving in our special needs community—both the young and the old— in their work places, in their schools and in their extracurricular activities. They are very proud of what they have and can accomplish. They are achieving greatness. We as parents are also very proud of them and are very grateful to them for having shared with us their inspirational work ethic and attitude.

# DON'T JUDGE A BOOK BY ITS COVER

It is only natural for us as humans to have certain prejudices when we first see something or someone. I suppose it's a learned trait as I just can't imagine that our human instincts would be prewired with prejudice. We hold prejudices towards most everything. Many of our prejudices are good, but many of them are not so good. Some are right and some are wrong. Some are simply just neutral. How many of you judged this book by its cover? I suppose most of you did.

I mention this because we often prejudge folks with special needs based on their disability. We do this at the time of the initial diagnosis, when we first meet someone with special needs, or when we first hear that someone has a particular disability. What is your initial reaction or thought when you hear the diagnosis of Down syndrome, Autism or Aspergers? I suspect that it is much like mine; not very positive, relatively speaking.

Furthermore, when you meet someone with a disability that affects their communication skills, what is your initial reaction? Again, I suspect it is much like mine; we believe their intellectual capabilities, as well as their opportunities to be productive and fruitful, are very limited. We often prejudge the learning and intellectual capabilities of people with special needs based on our initial introduction to their communication skills. My initial reaction would be that this is perfectly normal; but is it? If it is normal, then why is it?

We can all think of people who we've prejudged on their communication skills. We often predetermine their learning capabilities. In most cases, the result is insignificant, but for others, it can have lifelong effects. Because of our prejudice, we often make erroneous decisions on educational curriculums and expectations. We sometimes don't take the time to learn and understand how an individual communicates and processes information. We simply judge their learning ability based on the ability to communicate.

There are countless examples where individuals with low communication skills have been able to develop their intellectual ability and knowledge to the point where they have changed the world as we know it. Helen Keller is an example of someone who initially had very limited communication skills but was extremely smart and exceptionally gifted; her life story is well-documented.

Helen Keller was both deaf and blind as the result of an early childhood illness. Before any professional therapy, most of Helen's communication came in the form of throwing tantrums when she got angry and laughing uncontrollably when she was happy.

Many thought she should be institutionalized as they considered her only as someone who was deaf, blind and could not speak. Her parents, however, saw beyond her physical issues—they saw her potential. They solicited the help of a special school for the blind, hoping they could develop Helen's ability to communicate and thus tap into her learning potential.

One of the school's educators, Anne Sullivan, was asked to work with Helen. Anne was able to develop a unique communication system, which enabled Helen to grow and develop intellectually. Among many other things, Helen went to college, became a world activist for people with disabilities and assisted in the creation of the ACLU. All of this was accomplished after many people thought Helen Keller should be institutionalized simply because she had a difficult time communicating.

Though Kate and others with special needs may never match the great achievements of Helen Keller, the same principles apply to them. We can't prejudge them on their intellectually capabilities simply by their ability to communicate. They are amazingly brilliant. Just because they communicate their thoughts a bit differently doesn't mean they don't and can't understand a concept or idea.

When Kate learned how to operate the remote control at age four but had an extremely small vocabulary, we knew she had the ability to learn so much more. When Kate learned how to operate an IPad and IPhone but couldn't utter more than a four-or-five-word sentence, we knew the learning ability was there. Our challenge, as with all our kids, was and is, how do we get her to tell us what she knows, what she can learn and how best she can learn it.

We are continually seeking and using new therapies and teaching methods to find the best match for Kate's communication abilities. The better the match, the better we enable her to grow and develop her intellectual abilities. It is wonderful to see her unlock small parts of her intellectually universe each and every day.

We've had to learn how Kate communicates and processes information in order for us to see her vast intellectual potential. Many times when we're working with her on school assignments, we know that she understands the concepts but we can't get her to understand how we want that information delivered to us. We've come to realize that we must understand that she processes the information a bit differently, and that it is *our* job to understand and learn those differences and then modify the processes accordingly.

Sometimes this can be a simply modification to the learning process. When we are trying to help Kate memorize concepts in social studies, for example, it is obvious that she knows what we are trying to teach her but she just can't seem to process the information in the format that we want. For example, if we tell her the capital of Kentucky is Frankfort and then ask her to name the capital of Kentucky, she can't recall it. However, if we ask the question in the form of a multiple choice question, she gets the right answer every time. It's our responsibility to understand this and make the modifications.

Many of our prejudgments are based on our initial feedback or perceptions when we first are introduced to a person. It is only after we spend time gaining further insight that we gain the full understanding of what we are experiencing.

How often have we walked away without gaining full sight of the picture, person or situation? Did we make the wrong decision because we did not fully understand? Did we lose a great opportunity to grow and develop ourselves, another person, a community or even the world because we held a prejudice and totally misunderstood?

Someone's ability to communicate in no way represents their ability to learn. In fact, I would submit to you that an individual's learning capacity is greatly enhanced in many ways when they have a disability. I would submit that they involuntarily access a significantly different and often greater part of their brain to assist them in adapting to the special needs of their communication, thus expanding their learning capacity.

People with special needs are very smart and bright. They have a very large capacity to learn; and they will learn. After 12 plus years I should not be amazed at Kate's learning ability, but I am. I've come to realize that the amazement will always be there—not only with Kate, but with all my kids. The brain is a wonderful thing.

# WITH A SPECIAL NEED
# COMES A SPECIAL NEED

Several years ago, soon after we moved to Lexington, we received a call from a complete stranger asking us for a big favor. She had learned about our family though a mutual friend and wanted our help as some of her close friends had recently lost their adult daughter, Regina, who had Down syndrome. The caller expressed to us that it had been over four months since Regina's passing and the family was still grieving their loss. She felt that if we visited with them as a family then perhaps we could offer some solitude, comfort and peace. We agreed and scheduled a visit to their home with Kate.

It was shortly after Christmas and the New Year that we met them in their home just south of Lexington. We visited over a fresh baked apple pie and coffee, getting to know each other with some simply pleasantries. Theirs was a traditional family, with him being the main breadwinner and she being an excellent homemaker. They had one other child, an adult son, who had recently graduated and was working in the Lexington area. We felt very welcome in their home, and the bonding and rapport between us was immediate and mutual.

The story of their life with their daughter was touching and amazing, to say the least. They were able to share with us how the husband taught her how to dance by putting her feet on top of his while they waltzed around the room. They told us how Regina grew up and graduated from high school, how she earned her independence, learned how to stay at home by herself, helped with the cooking, performed chores, etc.

They shared with us their nighttime routines of dinner, relaxing, bedtime prayers and always a bedtime, "I love you," and hug. All of this was shared with us through many tears and heartache.

I could see and feel a difference in their grief and loss different from other's I have witnessed. I could feel there was something quite different about having to say goodbye and letting go of someone with special needs.

I remember having to say goodbye to Tommy at his funeral. There was a certain emptiness that I felt and still feel to this day. At the same time, there's a comforting solitude that he served His glory here on earth and he has a very special place now. I've lost a lot of loved one's over the years, but Tommy's loss is different. It's a difference that I can't explain. It is a difference that I continue to seek the wisdom to understand.

The same holds true when we have to let our loved ones with special needs grow and mature through life. My friend, Charles, whom you met earlier shared the experience of his son, Matthew, moving out of the house. Matthew had recently graduated from high school and had secured a good paying job in Lexington, about a 30-minute drive from their home in Winchester. Matthew had moved to Lexington and was living with a roommate. I thought, "WOW, mission accomplished!"

I mean, as a parent, isn't seeing our kids become self-sufficient, productive citizens the culmination of our life's work? I asked Charles how Matthew was doing and he said he was doing great. Matthew was making good money, enjoying his roommate and his newfound freedom and independence. I asked if there were any unforeseen issues and he said there was just one. Charles said he himself was going to pieces.

He said not having Matthew around the house was awful. Charles said his oldest daughter had moved out several years earlier and that wasn't a problem, but with Matthew it was different. He missed Matthew's companionship and the daily routines. He missed Matthew's smiling face and laughter each day. I think Matthew's dad was homesick, which is odd I guess, because he wasn't the one that left home . . . another one of life's peculiar quirks.

I had a similar conversation with a father who said his daughter with special needs was getting ready to go off to college a couple of hours away. I asked him how that was going and he said, "Not good." I asked why and he said he was having a really tough time letting her go. As a matter of fact, he said she was supposed to leave in January but he delayed it until the spring so he could spend a little more time with her. He just wasn't ready to let go.

I hear and experience these stories of having to let go and wonder about these feelings and emotions. I'm no psychologist, but I think it has something to do with need. You see, I think when we all have the instinct to be needed and when someone calls upon you to be care for their special needs, a special bond occurs. People with special needs certainly require a special need.

We as parents, family and friends graciously take on that responsibility. We love it and honor it. It's not that we love them more than our other kids or companions. It's not that we care about them more than we care about others. We love all our kids the same, but that special need to be needed triggers a special, nurturing bond between family, friends and community. When we have to let go, even though we know it is for the best, it hurts; it really hurts, but in a special way.

# THE PRISM OF DOWN SYNDROME

As I mentioned before, Kate has been a great teacher to us all. Through the years, Kate has taught us way more than we have taught her. These life lessons would have never been learned were it not for Kate and Down syndrome. I suppose we would have eventually learned them through some other life experience, seminar or book reading, but not nearly with the impact, veracity and scope with which they have been taught by Kate.

People are a lot like prisms—no two are the same. When the same light is shown through two prisms, the reflections and resulting lights are different.

Each of us acts as a prism. Life passes through each of us and we reflect uniqueness unlike any other person. Kate is one of my prisms through which many life experiences pass. As these experiences pass through Kate's prism, the reflections I see are quite different and unique.

There are many life lessons which I have learned from rearing Kate, ones that I lean on each day, and ones that I use as a foundation for future growth and development. These lessons have been learned because many of my life's experiences have passed through Kate. I'm sure these lessons would have been acquired otherwise, but through Kate, they have a different glow, a different aura and a different pattern about them.

Perseverance and having fun in life are two concepts that I see in a dramatically different light as a result of rearing Kate. These are simple, ordinary ideas and they've been a part of me for all my life, but since March 25, 2000, their meanings have changed a bit. You

119

see, I began seeing these concepts through a new and vibrant prism on the day that Kate was born.

Perseverance is one of those concepts that can be a bit confusing. Many people believe it's interchangeable with endurance, but the two have different meanings. According to Webster's dictionary, the definition of, "perseverance," is *"Steadfastness in doing something despite difficulty or delay in achieving success,"* where as the true definition of, "endurance" is, *"The capacity of something to last or to withstand wear and tear."*

Now, many people can endure but few can persevere. If you can't quite grasp the difference, let me try to explain. Marathon runners are considered endurance athletes. It's actually pretty easy to train and race if there's really no obstacle or challenge other than running to build your endurance. You simply train the body to endure the physical demands it takes to finish the race.

The majority of the population has the ability to complete a marathon, but less than one percent of the population ever does. The vast majority of people who set out to complete a marathon never do. Why? They do not have the perseverance. They simply can't persevere through all the obstacles that arise such as injuries, weather, time management or any other obstacle, and that's just to train for the race.

Many people may start the race and get halfway or more through the race and then give up. Most people can't persevere through the challenges and obstacles that arise, such as bad weather, cramps, blisters, etc. They've trained and have the endurance the endurance, but unforeseen challenges arise and they simply can't persevere.

I make this point because people with special needs often display amazing perseverance. As I've discussed, I grew up in sports and athletics, and still keep an active interest in them. The word and concept of perseverance has been a regular mantra that I've heard from coaches all of my life. It wasn't until Kate was born and Down syndrome was made part of my everyday life that I really understood what perseverance truly meant in terms of everyday living.

It wasn't until Kate entered our lives that I understood how this one fundamental characteristic was so vital and critical in determining the success of everyday life. In my mind, perseverance was only reserved for athletes. Perseverance was only applicable to those on the "battlefield." If you weren't an athlete, why did you need perseverance?

Kate and others with differing needs take on this race we call life with such vigor and enthusiasm each and every day. It would be so easy for them to make excuses and quit, but they refuse. They never back down from not only the regular challenges but also those additional challenges that face them as one who has a disability. These challenges would make most people fall to their knees and say no more, but they take them on with an attitude that makes everyone so proud.

You may be asking, what additional challenges? What additional obstacles? Let me share just a few:

- Could you get up and be excited for school or work if you knew your IQ was far less than your peers and everything you had to learn or do required a lot more time and energy?
- What would your attitude be like if you were never invited to be on the regular cheerleading team, sports team, academic team, dance team or chorale group?
- How would you feel if you knew you may never get to drive?
- How would you feel if you could not talk as well as others and the language barrier made it extremely difficult to communicate?

I don't know about you, but I would be hard-pressed to say that I would have the perseverance to face these obstacles. These challenges are what Kate and most people with a disability face each and every day along with life's normal challenges. Yet Kate, and many like her, takes on each day as if it were her last. Kate gets up, bounces out the door and greets her teachers and friends at school with a daily, "Hello," and a smile. She looks forward to her extracurricular activities and at the end of each day, she loves knowing that she gave it her best.

Seeing her do this is very inspiring to me as her father. Seeing her zesty attitude allows me to see my challenges and obstacles in a different light. Seeing her perseverance totally changes my paradigm. Perseverance is a character trait which we all need to grow and develop. It is one of the cornerstones of a strong foundation on which we will all rely upon for success

Having fun each day became a family mantra of ours several years ago. We always try to have a cheery disposition each day and we always seem to be up for a laugh and ready for some fun, but a sincere, concerted effort didn't really begin until Kate was about four years old and we started the, "Have Fun Today," code of conduct.

When Kate's school day was over, it became a habit for us to first ask her if she'd had fun that day. She'd say, "Yes," and then we would proceed with our other pleasantries and conversation.

Through the course of this ritual, Kate picked up on our regular dialogue and as she began to talk, she started greeting me at the door after a long days work with, "Dad, you're home! Did you have fun today?" We first found it humorous how she had adopted this conversation piece. We passed it off as a cute moment and didn't give it much thought. As the days, weeks and months passed, she continued her daily greeting to me.

I started thinking about that question a bit more as time and our ritual went on. When she was asked, you could tell she really was having fun during her day. When I was asked, I sometimes had to fake it. I finally started thinking, what if I could tell her that I really *did* have fun during my day. I made it a point to find some fun in each day, so I could truly say, "Yes," when she greeted me at the door with, "Dad did you have fun today?"

This doesn't mean that I have to have go-to-an-amusement-park type fun each day. It simply means that somewhere in my day, I truly need to have some fun. It may mean that I stop and have that latte, work with a better attitude or go have lunch in the park.

Fill each day with some joy and laughter. Have some fun each day. Kate does and it makes a world of difference in her life. It has taught me that life is too short not to have some fun each and every day. If you do the same, I promise your outlook and disposition on life will be much more positive and your days will be filled with much more joy. Now go have some fun!

# THE FUTURE FOR KATE

Throughout this short journey you've heard me say many times that Kate is really no different than our other kids, yet at the same time, I have shared many stories and instances where she is different. So which is it? Is she different or is she not? It's a very interesting question that I can only answer with this: "She is the same because she is different; she is different because she is not the same." With that, my vision for Kate and her future is really no different than what I hope for our other kids. So, what are my hopes for Kate and her future?

- *My hope is that she fulfills her own dreams and aspirations. She loves to dance and entertain. My hope is that she dances and entertains to the best of her abilities, bringing joy to those who see her perform.*
- *My hope is that she has a positive influence on everyone she meets, whether for just a chance meeting or for a long, enduring friendship.*
- *My hope is that she has the courage to take on each day as if it was her last, having a constant focus on what she can do versus what she can't do; recognizing and honoring her talents.*
- *My hope is that she continues to develop a strong relationship with God as this is the foundation upon which all else is built.*
- *My hope is that she continues to take pride in herself and everything that she accomplishes. My hope is that she understands that she has remarkable talents and she should be proud of who she is and what she can achieve.*
- *My hope is that she understands her capabilities and sets her expectations so she can realize them.*

- *My hope is that she continues to be an inspirational self-advocate for herself and for her peers who have different needs, lending yet another voice to express that they are people first—people who may have a diagnosis but are not simply that diagnosis.*

My job is to nurture our kids' dreams and aspirations. Kala and Kelsey have done an outstanding job of holding true to their hearts and roots as they determine who they would like to become and what they would like to do in their lives. They are extremely conscious of living a life of who you are versus what you do.

As for Kate, her dreams and aspirations are not much different than her sisters. One night we were picking up Kala for a dinner outing. As we were waiting for her, Kate said, "Dad, I want to go to college." A few years ago I would have dismissed it as something that was never going to happen. But I responded, "Well, you have to keep studying and doing well in school." She smiled the biggest smile and said, "I know, but school's really hard," to which I said, "Yes, it's hard for everybody." We've learned to not put any limitations on what she can accomplish, mainly because she has not put any limitations on herself.

I think we all worry to some extent about our kids' future, regardless of whether or not they have a disability. I think that's only natural for us as parents. It's impossible for us to peer into the future to see what it holds for any of our kids—what will they will do for a living, will they get married, where will they live, etc. These are all questions we just can't answer. To be honest I'm more concerned about the answers to these questions:

- Will our kids be kind and merciful to the less fortunate?
- Will they be generous with their charity?
- Will they give of their time to better their community, neighbors and society?

I'm more concerned with who they are rather than what they will become in life. I am not worried about what they are or what they will become—somehow that usually takes care of itself. We get so wrapped up in what we do for a living that we lose focus on what is at the heart of the matter, and that is who we are in life.

I want our kids to be considered good stewards of their charity and time. I want them to be good stewards of their hearts and their souls. I don't want them to be known for what they do for a living. I want them to be known for who they are, which is determined by how they treat others, how they give back to their neighbors and how they take care of their fellow citizens.

If each of our daughters can accomplish these objectives, I will have passed my little piece of the world off to very capable hands. I will have honored and fulfilled my responsibility of being a father and will lay down knowing that God's will has been done.

So, what does the future hold for you? Will you see the world a bit differently since our chance meeting here? If you do, it will make me smile; that was one of my goals. If you're expecting a child, I hope you have a bit more comfort and a bit less anxiety in wondering if your child will have a disability. If you are comforted, it makes me smile; that was one of my goals as well. And, if you've been given a diagnosis and you are scared, afraid and full of mixed emotions, I pray that you find the solitude and grace to accept your beautiful new child for who they are—a true gift and blessing from above that will bring untold joy and happiness in your life. If you do that, it will not only make me smile, but it will make others smile too; because that was my last, but most important, goal.

# APPENDIX

*Resources and references:*

Brighter Tomorrows project
www.brightertomorrows.org

Human Development Institute—University of Kentucky
www.hdi.uky.edu

National Down Syndrome Society
www.NDSS.org

Down Syndrome Association of Central Kentucky
www.DSACK.org

Down Syndrome Association of Louisville Kentucky
www.downsyndromeoflouisville.org

National Autism Association
www.nationalautismassociation.org

Autism Society of the Bluegrass
www.asbg.org